A selection of readi
The New T

with some psalms and

John Hedges
Taizé 1993

A selection of readings from

The New Testament

with some psalms and prayers

Fount
An Imprint of HarperCollins*Publishers*

Fount Paperbacks is an imprint of
HarperCollins*Religious*
Part of HarperCollins*Publishers*
77-85 Fulham Palace Road, London W6 8JB

First published in Great Britain
in 1993 by Fount Paperbacks

10 9 8 7 6 5 4 3 2 1

Originally published as *Textes choisis du Nouveau Testament,
quelques psaumes et des prières*
© 1992: Ateliers et Presses de Taizé,
71250 The Taizé Community, France
English translation © 1993: Ateliers et Presses de Taizé

A catalogue record for this book is
available from the British Library

ISBN 0 00 627703 9

Set in Bembo by Avocet Typesetters, Bicester, Oxon

Printed and bound in Great Britain by
HarperCollinsManufacturing Glasgow

Contents

Foreword

Who is this Jesus the Gospel speaks about?

He is the one of whom his disciple John writes, "Among you there is 'Someone' you do not know."

Who is this Christ Jesus?

Christ was in God, even before the universe began, from all eternity.

From the birth of humanity, he was the Living Word.

Then, humbly, he came among human beings.

If Jesus had not lived in our midst, God would seem far off and unreachable. But through his life on the earth, Jesus has allowed God to appear as he is.

And today, risen from the dead, the Christ lives in us through the Holy Spirit. Still more, he is united with every human being, without exception.

Perceptible to one, unrecognized by another, his mysterious presence is there always. It is as if we heard him say, "Do you not know that I am near you and that through the Holy Spirit I live in you? I will never leave you. Never."

Christ Jesus did not come to earth to judge the world, but so that through him every human creature should be saved – reconciled.

And yet it can happen that the human heart be possessed by a secret fear: God is going to punish me. Where does this feeling of being in the wrong come from, even in early childhood? To think that God punishes human beings is one of the greatest obstacles to faith.

When God is seen as a tyrannical judge, Saint John reminds us in letters of fire, "God is love . . . It is not we who loved God, it is God who loved us . . ."

Never, never indeed, is God a tormentor of the human conscience. He buries our past in the heart of Christ and has already taken care of our future. God comes to weave our life like a beautiful garment, with the warm threads of his compassion.

He tells each of us, "I know your trials and your poverty, and yet you have all that you could wish for."

And what do we have? His presence, always offered, source of freedom, hidden in the deepest part of ourselves.

And communion with him commits us in his name to lighten the distress of the innocent and to undertake responsibilities to reduce the human suffering on earth.

When we open the Gospel, each of us can say, "These words of Jesus are rather like a very ancient letter written in an unknown language. But since it is written to me by someone who loves me, I am going to try to understand its meaning, and to put into practice right away the little I have grasped."

Welcoming so many young people on our hill of Taizé all year long, and seeing their faces week after week – Mediterranean and Scandinavian, Portuguese and Slav, African and Asian faces – the brothers and I wonder, "Do these young people understand the Gospel when it is being read during the prayer services? Will they not be put off if some of the readings are too difficult to grasp?"

It is this preoccupation which has led us to publish a selection of readings from the New Testament. Two of the brothers have gathered together texts through which the reader may confidently seek to get right to the heart of the Gospel message.

Why a selection of texts and not the whole New Testament?

If we start by reading excerpts, we prepare ourselves little by little to grasp the New Testament in its entirety. Understanding progresses gradually.

Extensive knowledge is not important at the outset. In time that will be of great value. But it is through the heart, in the depths of themselves, that human beings begin to grasp the Mystery of Faith. Knowledge will come. Everything is not granted at once. An inner life is developed step by step. Today, more than in the past, we enter into the faith by going forward in stages.

Right at the depth of the human condition lies the longing for a presence, the silent desire for a communion. Let us never forget that this simple desire for God is already the beginning of faith.

Moreover, no one is able to understand the entire Gospel in isolation from others. Each person has to say, "In this unique communion which is the Church, what I do not understand of the faith is understood by others who are living from it. I do not rely on my faith alone but on the faith of Christians of all times, those who have gone before us, from the time of Mary and the apostles to those of today. And day after day I prepare inwardly to put my trust in the Mystery of Faith."

So it becomes clear that faith – trusting in God – is a very simple reality, so simple that everyone could receive it. It is like surging upwards again and again, a thousand times, throughout our life and until our very last breath.

BROTHER ROGER OF TAIZÉ

Note to the Reader

The word "gospel" means "good news". At the beginning of the New Testament, the four Gospels of Matthew, Mark, Luke and John tell of how Jesus came among human beings and describe certain events of his life, his death and his resurrection. They present these events as good news, as an amazingly liberating announcement from God.

Compared with the founders of the great religions, Jesus showed surprisingly little concern for the fate of his words. He did not write them down, nor did he apparently establish a precise formulation of them. However, the impact they produced was so strong that certain people remembered them and, in fact, the early believers eventually started to gather together the sayings of Jesus in written form. Yet it is not only his words that he leaves to human beings. As he says in Mark 10:45, he considered that his mission was to "give his life", and so it is that he offers to those who "follow him" the possibility of living from the love with which he loved them.

Finally, it was in the latter part of the first century that the large collections of texts which we know as "the Gospels" took the form in which we have them now. Each of the four has its own proper accent but all of them have the same intention: to make their readers understand Jesus as he was, and to bring him close to them through the telling of words and events that were part of his existence. We have chosen readings which make it possible to follow the various stages of Jesus's life.

To the readings from the Gospels, we have added some accounts from the beginning of the Book of the Acts of the

Apostles. These relate events which happened very soon after the death and resurrection of Jesus.

Next come passages from the Letters of Paul, James, Peter and John and from the Letter to the Hebrews, whose author is unknown. These Letters set out to show what Christians have to live in practical terms, in response to the good news announced by the Gospels.

If the choice of readings from the Letters is shorter than that from the Gospels, it is because the Letters contain long passages which deal with particular circumstances. We have preferred to choose only passages which are within the reach of as many people as possible and which are the least linked to the problems of a particular period in time. The excerpts from St Paul have been arranged according to themes.

Then comes a short selection from the psalms of the Old Testament. The psalms are the prayers of the Jewish people and Jesus himself prayed them. Indeed, so penetrated was he by them, that they sprang to his lips even on the cross. In turn, the psalms have nourished Christians' prayer from the very earliest times.

The reading of the Gospel has a very central place in the life of Taizé. The great diversity of language, culture and background among the young adults who join with the community for prayer leads to the choice, morning, noon and evening, of readings which are not too long and which can be readily grasped without explanation. Indeed, to help those who wish to nourish their daily life with the Word of God, the *Letter from Taizé* proposes a short Bible reading, easily accessible even to those who know little of the Bible, for each day of the year.

It is during the noon prayer, in the Church of Reconciliation, that Brother Roger reads a prayer which he has written for that particular day. Very often inspired by the reading for the day, these prayers attempt to express something of our reception of the Word of God and our response to it. A number of these prayers form the final section of the book.

When a passage from the Gospels is read while Christians are gathered for prayer, it is not merely in order to supply information concerning a distant Jesus belonging to the past. We listen to the Gospel in order to go and meet someone who is alive. By learning what he was, we learn what he is today. His words remain forever capable of transforming human existence.

The Church meets together constantly to listen to the Gospel. Every year, during its prayer cycle (the "liturgical year"), it retraces the way leading from the birth of Jesus to his public ministry and right on to his death and resurrection. In doing so, it is not simply reliving through imagination the progress of a certain earthly life that lasted over thirty years; it is in fact associating itself with that life and participating in it. Indeed, Jesus's words take on their full meaning only when they lead us to follow him.

The Gospel according to Matthew, Mark Luke and John

Childhood

John the Baptist's birth is foretold (LUKE 1:5-25)

In the days when Herod was king of Judea, there was a priest called Zechariah. His wife's name was Elizabeth. God knew them as just people who observed all the Lord's commandments and ordinances without fail. But they had no children, and it was thought that Elizabeth would never bear a child for both she and her husband were well on in years.

One day, Zechariah was carrying out his priestly duties after being chosen by lot to enter the Temple of the Lord and burn incense. Meanwhile all the faithful were praying outside. Then there appeared an angel of the Lord who stood on the right of the altar on which the incense was offered. At this sight, Zechariah was gripped by fear, but the angel told him, "Fear not, Zechariah, for your prayers have now been heard. Your wife will bear you a son whom you will name John. He will fill you with joy and delight, and many people will rejoice in his birth, for he will be great in the sight of God. He is not to drink wine or liquor. Right from his mother's womb he will be filled with the Holy Spirit, and he will bring back many believers to the Lord their God. Endowed with Elijah's spirit and power, he will open up a way for the Lord by reconciling parents with their children and rebels with the wisdom of the just – and so prepare for the Lord a people ready to receive him."

Zechariah asked the angel, "How can I be sure of this? Indeed I am an old man and my wife too is well on in years."

The angel answered him, "I am Gabriel, and I stand before God. I was sent to speak to you, and to bring you this good news. But since you have not believed my words, which will nevertheless be fulfilled in their proper time, you will be struck dumb and will not be able to speak until all this has happened."

Meanwhile the people were waiting for Zechariah to come out, and they were wondering what was delaying him. But when he did come out and could not speak to them, they grasped that he had seen a vision in the Temple. As for Zechariah, he could only make signs to them while remaining dumb. When his time of service was over, he went back home.

Shortly after this, Elizabeth became pregnant, and for five months she kept it secret; she told herself, "So this is what the Lord has done for me at the time when it has pleased him to deliver me from the humiliation I suffered among the people."

Jesus's birth is announced (LUKE 1:26–38)

Six months after John was conceived, the angel Gabriel was sent by God to a town of Galilee called Nazareth, to visit a virgin engaged to a man named Joseph, a descendant of King David. The virgin's name was Mary. The angel went to her home and greeted her, "Rejoice, O Filled-with-Grace! The Lord is with you." These words puzzled Mary greatly, and she wondered what the greeting meant. But the angel said to her, "Have trust, Mary, for God loves you. You will conceive and give birth to a child whom you will name Jesus. He will be great, and people will call him Son of the Most High. The Lord God will grant him his ancestor David's throne, and he will reign over the people of God for ever. His kingdom will have no end." Mary asked the angel, "How will this be possible since I am a virgin?" The angel answered, "The Holy Spirit will come, and the power of the Most High will cover you with its shadow so that the child will be holy and will be called the Son of God. Besides, in spite of her age, Elizabeth, your cousin, who was considered unable to bear children, has conceived a son and is now in her sixth month. Indeed nothing is impossible for God." Then Mary said, "Here am I as the Lord's servant. May what you have announced be done to me." And the angel left her.

Mary visits Elizabeth (LUKE 1:39–56)

At once Mary made haste to go to a town set in the Judean hill country. There she went into Zechariah's house and greeted Elizabeth. Now as soon as Elizabeth heard Mary's greeting, the child leapt in her womb. Filled with the Holy Spirit, Elizabeth exclaimed, "As no other woman, you are blessed, and blessed is the one to whom you will give birth! And how is it that my Lord's mother should visit me? For as soon as your greeting reached my ears, the child in my womb leapt for joy. Yes, blest are you for having believed in the fulfilment of the promise made to you from the Lord." Then Mary said,

"My soul proclaims the splendour of the Lord,
and my spirit rejoices in God my Saviour
who has taken into consideration
his servant's humble condition.
Yes, from now on, only blest shall I be called
throughout the ages,
for the Almighty has done marvels for me.
Holy is God's name, whose mercy will extend

from age to age to those who adore him.
Through the strength of his arm,
he has scattered the haughty hearts,
tumbled the seats of the powerful,
to raise up the humble.
On the hungry he has lavished good things in
plenty, but sent the rich away empty-handed.
Remembering his merciful love,
he has come to the aid of his servant people, Israel,
according to his promise to our ancestors,
to Abraham and his descendants
for ever."

Mary stayed about three months with Elizabeth, and then she
went home.

John the Baptist's birth (LUKE 1:57–68,80)

The day came for Elizabeth to give birth, and she brought
into the world a boy. When her neighbours and relatives learnt
that the Lord had shown her his merciful love, they shared
her joy. On the eighth day after the birth, they came for the
child's circumcision. They were going to name him Zechariah
after his father when his mother spoke up. "No," she said,
"he will be called John." They answered her, "But nobody
in your family is called by this name!" And they made signs
to his father to find out which name he wanted to give to
his son. Zechariah asked for a writing tablet and wrote down,
"His name is John." And they were all amazed. At this very
moment, he recovered his speech and started to praise God.
In the neighbourhood all were astounded, and these events
were retold throughout the Judean hill country. All who heard

of them were filled with awe and wondered, "What will become of this child?" for indeed the Lord's hand was with him.

Then his father Zechariah was filled with the Holy Spirit, and prophesied, "Blessed be the Lord God of Israel for visiting his people and setting them free." John grew up and his spirit developed. He lived in the wilderness until the day he appeared publicly to the people of Israel.

Jesus's birth (LUKE 2:1–20)

In those days Caesar Augustus decreed a census of all the inhabitants of the Roman Empire. This first census took place while Quirinius was governor of Syria. Everyone was to go and be registered in their place of origin. Joseph left the town of Nazareth in Galilee, and went to King David's town, Bethlehem in Judea, for he was descended from David and belonged to his house. Joseph went with Mary, to whom he was engaged and who was pregnant, so that she could be registered with him.

Now, while they were there, the day came for her to have her child. There was no room for them in the inn so they took shelter in a stable. Mary gave birth to her firstborn son, wrapped him up, and laid him in a manger – *where the cattle feed*.*

In the fields around, there were shepherds keeping watch over their flocks during the night. An angel of the Lord appeared to them and the glory of the Lord shone round about them. They were terrified. But the angel told them, "Fear not, for it is good news, a source of great joy for the whole

---

* In order to develop the meaning more fully, a number of short insertions have been introduced into the text. These are shown in italics.

people, that I am bringing you. This day, in David's town, to you is born a Saviour who is Christ and Lord. You will find him as a newborn child, wrapped up and lying in a manger. This is the sign I am giving you!" And suddenly the angel was joined by a great multitude from heaven, praising God with these words, "Glory to God in the highest, and on earth peace to his beloved!"

Once the angels had gone back to heaven, the shepherds said to one another, "Let us go to Bethlehem and see this event the Lord has made known to us." They set off without delay, and found Mary and Joseph and the newborn child lying in the manger. When they saw this, the shepherds repeated what had been said to them about the child, and all who heard it marvelled at what they were saying. As for Mary, she treasured all these memories, and pondered them in her heart. The shepherds went back, glorifying and praising God for all they had heard and seen in accordance with what they had been told.

Jesus is presented in the Temple (LUKE 2:21-39)

After eight days, when the child was circumcised, he was called Jesus, the name given by the angel who appeared to Mary. Then came the day for their purification in keeping with the Law of Moses. Joseph and Mary took the child to Jerusalem to present him to the Lord – for it is written in the Law of the Lord that every firstborn boy must be consecrated to the Lord – and, also according to the Law, to offer in sacrifice "a pair of turtledoves or two young pigeons".

Now in Jerusalem there was a man called Simeon. He was a just and devout man who was waiting fervently for the Christ that the Lord had promised for the consolation of Israel. The Holy Spirit rested on him and had revealed to him that he would

not die before seeing the Christ of the Lord. Prompted by the
Spirit, he went to the Temple, and when the parents brought
in the child Jesus to do for him what was prescribed by the
Law, Simeon took him in his arms, and blessed God, saying,

> "Now, O Lord, you let your servant depart in peace
> according to your promise. For indeed my eyes have seen
> your salvation, prepared in the presence of all peoples –
> a light to reveal you to the nations and to glorify Israel
> your people."

As the child's parents marvelled at what was being said about
him, Simeon blessed them and said to Mary his mother, "Look,
this child is destined to cause the falling down and the rising
up of many in Israel, and to be a sign that will be opposed
– so that the thoughts of many hearts may be revealed. As for
you, a sword will pierce your soul also."

In the Temple, there was also Anna, a prophetess. She was
quite old, having married young and lived with her husband
for seven years before becoming a widow. She was now eighty-
four. She never left the Temple but worshipped God night
and day, fasting and praying. She came up at that very moment,
and began to praise God and to speak about the child to all
who were looking forward to the deliverance of Jerusalem.

The wise men from the East (MATTHEW 2:1–12)

After Jesus was born at Bethlehem of Judea in the days of King
Herod, wise men from the East came to Jerusalem and asked,
"Where is the newborn king of the Jews? We have seen his
star rising in the East, and have come to worship him." This
news disturbed King Herod, as well as all Jerusalem. He called

together all the chief priests and the legal experts and asked them where the Christ was to be born. "At Bethlehem in Judea," they answered, "for this is what one of the prophets has written: 'And you, O Bethlehem, you are certainly not the least of Judea's chief towns, for from you will come out the shepherd of my people Israel.' " So Herod summoned the wise men secretly, and inquired from them the precise date when the star had appeared. Then he sent them to Bethlehem. "Go and find out everything concerning this child," he told them. "When you have found him, let me know so that I too may go and worship him."

Having listened to the king, the wise men set out, and the star they had seen rising went ahead of them until it stopped above the place where the child was. At the sight of the star they were overwhelmed with joy. They went into the house, saw the child with Mary his mother, fell on their knees, and worshipped him. Then, opening their treasures, they presented him with gifts of gold, frankincense and myrrh. In a dream, they were warned by God not to return to Herod; so they went back to their country by another way.

The flight to Egypt (MATTHEW 2:13–16, 19–23)

After the wise men had left, an angel of the Lord appeared to Joseph in a dream and told him, "Get up, take the child and his mother, and flee to Egypt. Remain there until I tell you to come back, for Herod intends to search for the child in order to get rid of him." That very night, Joseph got up, took the child and his mother, and went with them to Egypt, where they remained until Herod's death. This was to fulfil what had been said by the Lord through one of the prophets, "Out of Egypt I called my son."

Livid with rage for having been tricked by the wise men, Herod sent his people to Bethlehem and its surroundings to slaughter all the male children up to two years old, according to the precise date he had obtained from the wise men.

At the time of Herod's death, an angel of the Lord appeared in a dream to Joseph in Egypt and told him, "Get up, take the child and his mother, and go back to the land of Israel, for those who were after the child's life are now dead." So Joseph got up, took the child and his mother and went back to his country. But when he learnt that Archelaus had succeeded his father on the throne of Judea, he was afraid to go there, and having been warned in a dream, they went to Galilee and settled down in a town called Nazareth, fulfilling what the Lord had said through one of the prophets, "He will be called the Nazarene."

At the age of twelve, Jesus goes up to the Temple (LUKE 2:40–52)

As the child Jesus developed and grew strong, filled with wisdom, God's love was with him.

Every year his parents went to Jerusalem for the Passover festival. When Jesus was twelve years old, they went up as usual. Once the festival was over, they started on their way back, but without being aware that their child had stayed behind in Jerusalem. They assumed that he was somewhere in the caravan, and they walked a whole day before starting to look for him among their relatives and friends. But when they did not find him, they returned to Jerusalem to continue their search there.

It was three days later that they found him in the Temple, seated among the doctors of the Law, listening to them and asking them questions. All who heard him were amazed at his discernment and his answers. When his parents saw him, they were very upset, and his mother asked him, "My child, why have you done this to us? See how worried your father and I have been, searching for you!" He answered them, "But why were you searching for me? Did you not know that I must be in my Father's house?" But they did not understand what he was talking about.

Then Jesus went back with them to Nazareth. He showed respect for their authority, and his mother treasured all these memories in her heart. Jesus grew up in wisdom, stature and love in the sight of God and people.

The Calling from God

John the Baptist (MATTHEW 3:1–11)

In due course, John the Baptist appeared in the desert of Judea where he preached, "Repent – *that is, turn your hearts towards God and turn away from evil* – for the kingdom of heaven has drawn near." He was the one whom the prophet Isaiah had spoken about with these words, "A voice cries in the desert: Prepare a way for the Lord, make his paths straight." This John wore a camel-hair garment and a leather loincloth; and his food was locusts and wild honey.

From Jerusalem, all of Judea and the whole of the Jordan valley, people came out to him and, confessing their sins, they were baptized by him in the Jordan river. But when he saw many Pharisees and Sadducees coming to be baptized – *they could be more self-assured than other believers* – he told them, "You vipers' brood! Who warned you about the coming wrath? Bear fruit in keeping with turning to God, and do not dare to tell yourselves, 'We have Abraham as our father', for I tell you, God is able to make sons of Abraham appear out of these stones. As from now the axe is laid at the root of the trees so that any tree that does not produce good fruit will be cut down and thrown into the fire. As for me, I baptize you in water so that you turn to God, but after me is coming he who is mightier than I, and whose sandals I am not worthy to take off: he will baptize you in the fire of the Holy Spirit."

Jesus's baptism (MATTHEW 3:13–17)

Then Jesus appeared, coming from Galilee. He went to John to be baptized by him in the Jordan. But John tried to talk him out of it, "It is I," he said, "who should be baptized by you, and here you come to me!" But Jesus answered him, "Let it now be so, for in this way we fulfil the will of God." So John agreed. Once he had been baptized, Jesus came up from the water, the heavens opened, and he saw the Spirit of God coming down like a dove and alighting on him, while a voice from heaven said, "This is my Son, my Beloved, in him my heart rejoices."

Jesus is tempted (MATTHEW 4:1–11)

Then Jesus was led by the Holy Spirit into the desert to be tested by the devil. After fasting for forty days and forty nights, he was hungry. The tempter appeared and said to him, "If you are the Son of God, order these stones to turn into bread." But he answered, "It is written *in the Scriptures:* Human beings do not live only on bread, but also on every word coming out of God's mouth."

Then the devil took him to the holy city, set him on the highest point of the Temple, and told him, "If you are the Son of God, throw yourself down, for it is written: He has commanded his angels to guard you, and they carry you in their arms lest you stumble against a stone." Jesus replied, "It is also written: Do not put the Lord your God to the test."

Again the devil took him, and set him on a very high mountain from where he showed him all the kingdoms of the world and their splendour. "All these," he told him, "I will give you, if you fall down at my feet and worship me." Then

Jesus said, "Out of my sight, Satan! for it is written: You will worship the Lord your God and no one else." So the devil left him, and behold angels came and took care of him.

Peter's catch (LUKE 5:1–11)

One day, by the lake of Gennesaret, Jesus was pressed on all sides by a crowd eager to listen to the word of God. He caught sight of two boats hauled up on the shore. The fishermen had got out of them and were cleaning their nets. He got into one of the boats – it was Simon's – and asked him to put out a little way from the shore. Then, seated in the boat, he taught the people.

When he had finished speaking he told Simon, "Put out into deep water, and let down your nets." Simon answered, "Master, we have worked hard all night long without catching anything, but since you say so, I will let down the nets." Having done this, they caught such a large number of fish that their nets began to tear, and they signalled to their companions in the other boat to come to their help. And they did so. They filled up both boats to the point where they began to sink.

When Simon Peter saw this, he fell down at Jesus' knees. "Go away from me, Lord," he said, "for I am a sinner!" Indeed their catch had absolutely startled him and all his companions, and likewise James and John, Zebedee's sons, who were Simon's partners. But Jesus told him, "Fear not. From now on you will be catching people." And after bringing their boats ashore, they left everything and followed him.

Jesus's Teaching

The Beatitudes (MATTHEW 4:23–5:16)

Jesus went throughout Galilee, teaching in the synagogues, preaching the joyful news of the kingdom of God, and healing all diseases and sicknesses among the people. And so his reputation spread throughout Syria, and all the sick and those suffering from various ailments – the possessed, the epileptics, the invalids – were brought to him, and he cured them. Large crowds started to follow him, coming from Galilee, the Decapolis, Jerusalem, Judea and from beyond the Jordan.

Seeing the crowds, Jesus went up a hill and sat down. His disciples came to him, and he began to teach them:

Blest are the poor in heart!
  theirs is the kingdom of heaven.
Blest are the sorrowful!
  they will be comforted.
Blest are the gentle!
  they will inherit the earth.
Blest are the hungry and thirsty for justice!
  they will receive it in plenty.
Blest are those who live in mercy!
  they will have it shown to them.
Blest are the clear hearts!
  they will see God.
Blest are the peacemakers!
  they will be known as God's children.

Blest are the persecuted for justice's sake!
  theirs is the kingdom of heaven.

"Blest are you when you are abused, persecuted, and slandered
for my sake, in all sorts of ways. Rejoice, exult, for great will
be your reward in heaven. This is indeed how the prophets
were persecuted before you.

"You are salt for the earth. But if salt loses its saltness, how
will it be made salty again? It is only good to be thrown away,
and to be trampled under foot.

"You are light for the world. And a town set on the top
of a hill cannot be hidden. Nor do people light up a lamp
to place it under an overturned vessel. No, they will put it
on a stand from where it will give light to all who are in the
room. In the same way must your light shine, so that people
may see the good you are doing, and give thanks for it to your
Father who is in heaven."

The law of the new covenant (LUKE 6:27–38,41–42)

"To you who hear me, I say: Show love to your enemies!
Do good to those who hate you! Bless those who curse you!
Pray for your slanderers! To whoever strikes you on one cheek,
present the other one! To whoever takes your coat, do not
refuse your shirt! To those who ask, give! From those who
take your goods, ask nothing back! Do for others, what you
wish them to do for you!

"If you love those who love you, what credit can you
expect? Even sinners love those who love them. And if you
do good to those who do good to you, what credit can you
expect? Even sinners do the same. And if you lend to those
from whom you hope for a profit in return, what credit are

you to expect? Even sinners lend to sinners who pay them back the same way.

"That is why you are to love your enemies and to do them good, to lend without hoping they will do the same for you. You will gain greatly by this and be the children of the Most High, for he is kind to the ungrateful and the selfish.

"Just like your Father, be compassionate. Judge not, and you will not be judged. Condemn not, and you will not be condemned. Forgive, and you will be forgiven. Give, and good measure, pressed down, shaken together, brimming over, will be poured out for you. Indeed the measure you give is the measure you will receive.

"Why do you observe a speck in the eye of your brother or sister without paying attention to the log in your own eye? And how can you say, 'Friend, let me take that speck out of your eye' while you yourself do not even see the log in your own eye? You hypocrite, start by taking the log out of your eye, and then you will see clearly to take out the speck from your companion's eye."

Basic attitudes (MATTHEW 6:5–13,16–34; 7:7–11)

"When you pray, do not do like the hypocrites; for they love to pray while standing in the synagogues and at the street corners so that they may be seen by other people. I tell you, they have already received their reward. As for you, when you pray, go to your room and close the door; then pray to your Father who is in that secret place. Your Father who sees what is done in secret will reward you.

"In your prayers do not heap up meaningless phrases as the Gentiles do, *that is, those who do not belong to the people of Israel*, for they think they will be heard all the better for their many words. Do not be like them, for your Father knows what you need even before you ask him for it.

"So pray this way:

Our Father in heaven, may your name be held holy.
May your kingdom come, and may your will *of love* be done on earth as it is in heaven.
Give us today our daily bread. Forgive us our sins as we forgive those who have sinned against us. Save us from temptation, and deliver us from evil.

"When you fast, do not look sad like the hypocrites do when they put on a grief-stricken air to let people know they are fasting. I tell you, they have already received their reward. But when you fast, anoint your head and wash your face, so that your fasting may be seen, not by others, but by your Father who is in secret; and your Father who sees in secret – *and knows what your heart intends* – will reward you.

"Do not store up treasures for yourselves on earth, where insects and rust destroy them and where thieves break in and steal them. But lay up treasures for yourselves in heaven, where there are neither insects nor rust nor burglars. For where your treasure is, there too is your heart.

"The eyes serve as a lamp for the body, so that if your eyes are clear, your whole body is full of light. But if your eyes do not see clearly, your whole body will be in darkness. If then the light in you is darkness, how obscure it will be!

"No one can serve two masters: for you will hate the one and love the other, you will be devoted to the one and laugh at the other. You cannot serve both God and money.

"Therefore, I tell you, neither to worry about your life for what you will eat and drink, nor about your body for what you will wear. Is not life more than nourishment, and the body more than clothing? Look at the birds in the sky: they neither sow nor reap nor gather into barns, yet they get their food from their heavenly Father. Are you not more valuable than they are? And can any of you by worrying add anything at all to the length of your life? And why do you worry about clothing? Observe how the lilies grow in the fields: they neither labour nor spin, and yet, I tell you, Solomon in his most splendid royal robes was not clothed like one of them. So if that is how God clothes the flowers of the field which are fresh today and tomorrow will be burnt, will he not take much better care of you, O people of little faith? So do not worry and wonder, 'What shall we eat? What shall we drink? How shall we dress?' It is the Gentiles who fret about these things. Your heavenly Father knows that you need them. So above all look for his kingdom and his justice, and all these things will be yours as well.

"Do not be anxious about tomorrow. Tomorrow will look after itself. Let today's trouble be enough!

"Ask, you will receive. Search, you will find. Knock, the door will be opened to you. For whoever asks receives, whoever searches finds, whoever knocks will have the door opened for them. Is there anyone among you who would give a stone when your child asks for bread? Or if the child asks for fish, would give a snake? If you then, evil as you are, know how to give what is good to your children, how much more will your heavenly Father give good things to those who ask him!"

Ministry and Parables

Jesus heals a paralytic (MARK 2:1–12)

Jesus went to Capernaum. It became known which house he was in, and so many people gathered there that there was no room left, even near the door.

Jesus was teaching when some people brought a paralytic carried by four men; but they could not get near Jesus because of the crowd. So they made an opening in the roof above Jesus, and let down the stretcher on which the paralytic was lying. Seeing this act of faith, Jesus said to the paralytic, "My son, your sins are forgiven."

Now some legal experts were sitting there, wondering in their hearts, "How can this man speak in such a way? It is blasphemy, since God alone can forgive sins!" At once, aware of the questioning which troubled them, Jesus told them, "Why all this grumbling in your hearts? Which is easier to say to the paralytic, 'Your sins are forgiven', or 'Rise up, pick up your stretcher, and walk'? Well, so that you may know that the Son of man has authority on earth to forgive sins, I order you," he said to the paralytic, "rise up, pick up your stretcher, and go home!" And in front of everybody, the man got up, picked up his stretcher, and went out of the house, while they all marvelled and praised God, saying, "We have never seen such a thing!"

The calling of Matthew (MATTHEW 9:9–13)

As Jesus was on his way from there, he saw a man sitting at

the tax collector's office. His name was Matthew. Jesus told him, "Follow me." He got up and followed him.

While Jesus sat at table in Matthew's house, many tax collectors and sinners came and sat down with him and his disciples. When the Pharisees saw this happening, they asked Jesus's disciples, "Why does your master eat with tax collectors and sinners?" Jesus overheard them and replied, "It is not the healthy who need a doctor but the sick. Go and learn what these words mean, 'It is mercy that pleases me, not sacrifice', for indeed I have not come to call the righteous, but sinners."

A question of fasting (MATTHEW 9:14-17)

Then John's disciples came to him, and asked, "Why do we and the Pharisees fast, while your disciples do not?" Jesus replied, "At a wedding the guests enjoy themselves as long as the bridegroom is with them. But days will come when the bridegroom will be taken away from them, and then they will fast. Besides, nobody patches up an old garment with a piece of unshrunken cloth, for when it is being washed the patch will pull away, and the tear becomes larger still. Neither is new wine poured into old wineskins, for the skins will burst, the wine run out, and the skins will be lost. No, the new wine is poured into new skins so that both are preserved."

The appointment of the twelve apostles (MARK 3:13-19)

Jesus went up a hill, and called to him those he wanted. They joined him. Then he appointed twelve whom he named apostles, and who were to be his companions, and to be sent out on mission to proclaim the good news, and to have power to drive out demons. These twelve were: Simon, to whom he gave the name Peter, James and John, Zebedee's sons whom he named Boanerges (which means Sons of Thunder), Andrew, Philip, Bartholomew, Matthew, Thomas, James son of Alphaeus, Thaddaeus, Simon the partisan, and Judas Iscariot, who was to betray Jesus.

The gift of living water (JOHN 4:3–31, 34–38)

To get to Galilee from Judea, Jesus had to pass through Samaria. On his way he came to a Samaritan town called Sychar, near the field that Jacob gave to his son Joseph. That was the place where Jacob's well was, and Jesus, tired from the journey, sat down by the well. It was around midday.

A Samaritan woman came to draw water. "Give me some to drink," asked Jesus, for his disciples had gone to town to buy food. The Samaritan woman answered him, "How is it that you, a Jew, ask me, a Samaritan woman, for a drink?" Indeed, Jews would have nothing to do with Samaritans. "If only you knew what God is offering," Jesus replied, "and who is the one who is asking you, 'Give me a drink', it would have been you who would have asked instead, and he would have given you living water." The woman said, "But you have nothing to draw with, and this well is so deep! Where do you draw the living water from? Are you greater than our ancestor Jacob who gave us this well and drank from it, together with his family and his cattle?" Jesus answered, "All who drink this water will be thirsty again, but whoever drinks the water I shall give will never be thirsty again, for that water will become in them like a spring pouring forth into eternal life." The woman asked, "Lord, give me that water so that I may not be thirsty, nor have to come back here to draw water."

"Go and call your husband," Jesus told her, "then come

back here." She answered, "I have no husband." Jesus said to her, "You are right in saying, 'I have no husband,' for you have had five husbands, and the man you are living with now is not your husband. So you did tell me the truth." The woman exclaimed, "Lord, I can see that you are a prophet! Our ancestors worshipped God on this mountain, whereas you Jews say that it is in Jerusalem that people should worship . . ." Jesus answered, "Believe me, woman, soon it will no longer be either on this mountain or in Jerusalem that people will worship the Father. You worship without knowing; we worship with full knowledge, for salvation comes from the Jews. But very soon – indeed right away – the real worshippers will worship the Father in the Spirit and in truth, for such is the kind of worshippers the Father is looking for. God is Spirit. Therefore, it is in the Spirit and in truth that he should be worshipped." The woman said, "I know the Messiah – that is, the Christ – will be coming to explain everything to us." Jesus replied, "I am he, the one speaking to you."

At this point his disciples came back and they were surprised to find him talking with a woman. Yet none of them asked him, "What do you want from her?" or "What are you speaking about with her?" As for the woman, leaving her water jar, she ran back to the town and announced, "Come and see a man who told me all I have ever done! Could he not be the Christ?" Straight away the people came out of the town and went to Jesus.

Meanwhile the disciples were urging Jesus to eat some food. He told them, "I find my food in fulfilling the will of the one who sent me, and in completing his work. Are you not in the habit of saying, 'Four more months, and it will be harvest time?' Well, I tell you, lift up your eyes, and look at the fields. Right now they are ready for harvesting! Already the harvester is receiving his wages! Already he is storing up his harvest for eternal life, so that sowers and harvesters are rejoicing together! For here the saying is confirmed, 'The one sows, the other reaps.' I have sent you to harvest where you have not laboured; others laboured, and you have benefited from their labour."

The faith of the centurion (LUKE 7:1–10)

When he had been speaking for a long time to many people, Jesus entered Capernaum. In the town there was a Roman officer whose rank was centurion. Now he had a servant who was dear to him and who was sick and about to die. Having heard of Jesus, the centurion sent him some Jewish notables, to ask him to come and heal his servant. When they came to Jesus they spoke earnestly in favour of the centurion, "He deserves to have you do this for him," they said, "for he loves our people, and he had our synagogue built." So Jesus went with them.

He was not far from the house when the centurion sent some friends to tell him, "Lord, do not trouble yourself to come under my roof, for I am not worthy; it is for this reason that I did not presume to come to you myself. But only say one word, and my servant will be cured. For I, a mere subaltern, have soldiers under my orders, and when I tell one, 'Go!' he goes, and another one, 'Come!' he comes, and say to my servant, 'Do this!' and he does it." Jesus marvelled when he heard the centurion's words, and turning around to face the crowd which was following him, he said, "I tell you, not even in Israel have I found such faith." When they came back to the centurion's house, his friends found the servant in perfect health.

The widow of Nain's son (LUKE 7:11–17)

Soon afterwards Jesus went with his disciples and a large crowd to a town called Nain. As he got near the town gate, there was a dead man, a widow's only son, who was being carried out to be buried. The widow was surrounded by a large number of the town's people. When the Lord saw her, he had compassion on her, and said to her, "Do not weep." Then he went and laid his hand on the bier, and those carrying it stood still. He said, "Young man, I tell you, rise up!" The dead man sat up and started speaking. Jesus gave him back to his mother.

Everyone was filled with awe, and they glorified God, exclaiming, "A great prophet has arisen among us!" and "God has visited his people!" And these words about Jesus spread through all Judea and the surrounding region.

Jesus calms a storm (MARK 4:35–41)

One evening, near the lake, Jesus said to his disciples, "Let us go across to the other side." Leaving the crowd behind, they took him in a boat and other boats were with him. A great storm arose, and the waves broke into the boat so that it was filling very quickly with water. Jesus was asleep in the stern, with his head on a cushion. They woke him up, saying, "Master, do you not care if we perish?" Jesus woke up and scolded the wind, telling the waves, "Calm down! Silence!" And the wind dropped, giving way to a great calm. Then he said to them, "Why are you frightened? Have you no faith?" Stricken with awe, they asked one another, "Who is this? Even the wind and the waves obey him!"

Jairus's daughter (MARK 5:22-24,35-43)

When a synagogue leader named Jairus saw Jesus, he fell at his feet, and implored him earnestly, "My little daughter is about to die. Come, I beg you, and lay your hands on her so that she may be healed and live." So Jesus went with him, and a large crowd followed, pressing all around him.

As they were on their way, people arrived from the synagogue leader's house and told him, "Your daughter is dead. Why bother the Master any further?" But Jesus paid no attention to their words and said to Jairus, "Fear not. Only believe." And he allowed no one to come with him except Peter and the two brothers, James and John. When they arrived at the synagogue leader's house, Jesus saw a great commotion, with people weeping and wailing loudly. He went in, and told them, "Why all this tumult and this weeping? The child is not dead but sleeping." They laughed at him. But he put them all out, and took with him the father and mother as well as his three disciples, and went into the room where the child was.

Taking the child by the hand, he said to her, "*Talitha kum!*" which means, "Little girl, I tell you to get up." At once the girl got up – she was twelve years old – and began to walk about. They were all overcome with amazement. Jesus ordered them not to speak about it to anybody, and to give the child something to eat.

The mystery of the Kingdom
(MATTHEW 11:16-19,25-30)

Jesus spoke to the crowd, "What comparison can be found to describe this generation's attitude? It is like children sitting in the market place and calling to each other, 'We have played the flute for you, but you would not dance! We have sung dirges for you, but you would not mourn!' For indeed John the Baptist came, neither eating nor drinking, and people said, 'He is completely crazy.' Then the Son of man came, eating and drinking, and people said, 'See that glutton, that drunkard, a friend of tax collectors and sinners!' However, wisdom is justified by her deeds."

Then Jesus went on, saying, "I praise you, Father, Lord of heaven and earth, for, while the mysteries of the Kingdom remain hidden from the wise and the experts, you reveal them to little children. Yes, Father, for in this your heart rejoices.

"All things have been entrusted to me by my Father, and no one knows the Son but the Father, and no one knows the Father but the Son and anyone to whom the Son chooses to reveal him.

"Come to me, all you who labour and are overburdened, I shall offer you relief. Take on my yoke, and learn from me, for I am gentle and humble in heart, and by me your souls will find relief. For my yoke does not bruise, nor my burden weigh down."

Jesus feeds five thousand people (MARK 6:30–44)

On their return from a mission, the apostles gathered around Jesus and told him all that they had done and taught. He said to them, "Come by yourselves to a remote place so that you can rest a little." For there was so much coming and going around them that they did not find time even to eat. So they went by boat to a remote place where they would be by themselves. But many people saw them going and realized what they were doing; from every town people hurried on foot to the place and got there before Jesus and his disciples. As Jesus went ashore, he saw a large crowd and felt compassion for them because they were like sheep without a shepherd. So he began to teach them at some length.

It was getting late. His disciples came to him and pointed out, "We are in a remote place and it is late now. Send these people away so that they can go to farms and villages and buy themselves something to eat." Jesus replied, "It is for you to give them something to eat." They said to him, "It would take an enormous amount of money even to give them a little bread to eat." Jesus asked them, "How many loaves have you got? Go and see." When they had done so, they said, "Five loaves and two fish." Then he ordered them to make everybody sit down in groups on the green grass, and they did so by hundreds or fifties. Then he took the five loaves and the two fish, looked up to heaven, gave thanks and said the blessing. And he broke the loaves, and gave them to his disciples to share out. In the same way he shared out the two fish among them all. Everyone ate to their fill. Twelve baskets were filled with scraps of bread and fish. Those who had eaten were more than five thousand.

Jesus walks on the water (MATTHEW 14:22–23)

Jesus made the disciples get into the boat immediately and go on ahead of him to the other side of the lake while he himself sent the crowds away. After this, he went up a hill to pray by himself. When evening came, he was there alone, while the boat was far from land, tossed by the waves, for the wind was contrary.

A little before dawn, Jesus came towards his disciples, walking on the lake waters. When they saw him, they were terrified. "It is a ghost," they said, and they cried out in fear. But Jesus told them at once, "Take courage! It is I. Do not be frightened." It was Peter who replied, "Lord, if it is you indeed, tell me to come to you on the water." And Jesus said, "Come!" So Peter got out of the boat and started walking on the lake towards Jesus. But the strength of the wind frightened him and he began to sink. So he cried out, "Lord, save me!" Jesus reached out his hand at once, caught him, and said to him, "O man of little faith, why did you doubt?" When they got into the boat, the wind dropped. Those who were in the boat bowed down before him, saying, "It is true, you are the Son of God."

Jesus heals a deaf-and-dumb person (MARK 7:32–37)

One day, they brought to Jesus a deaf man who also had a speech impediment, and they asked him to lay his hands on him. Taking the man aside, away from the crowd, Jesus put his fingers into the man's ears and touched his tongue with spittle. Then he looked up to heaven, sighed, and told him, "Ephphatha", that is, "Open up". At once his ears were opened, his tongue became untied, and his speech was clear. Jesus ordered them to tell nobody what had happened, but the more he insisted, the more they spoke about it. They were filled with wonder beyond measure, and they said, "All that he does is good, he makes the deaf hear and the dumb speak."

The Transfiguration (MATTHEW 17:1–9)

A few days later, Jesus took with him Peter, James and his brother John, and led them up a high mountain, on their own. In their presence he was transfigured – his face was shining like the sun, and his clothes became as dazzling as light.

Suddenly there appeared to them Moses and Elijah, conversing with Jesus. Then Peter said to Jesus, "Lord, how wonderful it is to be here! If you wish, I shall put up three tents, one for you, one for Moses, and one for Elijah." He was still speaking when a bright cloud enveloped them, and from the cloud a voice said, "This is my Son in whom is all my love; in him my heart rejoices; listen to him." At the sound of the voice, the disciples were filled with awe, and they fell face downwards on the ground. But Jesus came and touched them, saying, "Rise up. Do not be frightened." And when they looked up, they saw no one but Jesus alone.

As they were going down the mountain, Jesus gave them this order, "Tell no one about this vision until the Son of man has risen from the dead."

The parable of the unmerciful debtor
(MATTHEW 18:21–35)

One day, Peter asked Jesus, "Lord, how many times am I to forgive someone who has wronged me? Up to seven times?" Jesus answered, "No, not up to seven times, but up to seventy times seven.

"For here is the way things work in the kingdom of heaven. There was a king who wanted to settle his accounts with his stewards. Right away they brought him one of them who owed several millions. Now this man had no means of paying back the sum. So his master ordered him to be sold, together with his wife, his children, and all his possessions. But the steward threw himself at the king's feet, begging, 'Lord, be patient with me, and I will pay you back all I owe you.' Moved with compassion for him, the master cancelled the debt and let him go.

"As the steward went out, he met one of his colleagues who owed him a small amount of money. He seized him by the throat, saying, 'Pay me back what you owe me!' His colleague fell at his feet, begging, 'Be patient with me, and I will pay you back.' But he did not listen and instead had him thrown into prison until he would pay back his debt.

"Their colleagues had seen what had happened. They were very sorry about it and they went and told their master the whole story. The master sent for the guilty man and told him, 'You wicked steward! I cancelled all your debt when you begged me. Should you not have been moved with compassion for your colleague just as I was for you?' Indignant, his master handed him over to the gaolers so that he be kept in prison until he paid back his whole debt. So this is how my heavenly Father will deal with you too, if you do not forgive one another from the bottom of your hearts."

The parable of the good Samaritan (LUKE 10:25–37)

On one occasion a doctor of the Law asked Jesus in order to test him, "Lord, what must I do to inherit eternal life?" Jesus told him, "What is written in the Law? What do you read in it?" He answered, "You shall love the Lord your God with all your heart, with all your soul, with all your strength, and with all your mind, and the other person just like yourself." Jesus told him, "You have answered right. Do this, and you have eternal life."

But he wanted to justify his inquiry, so he asked Jesus, "And who is this other person?" Jesus answered, "A man was going down from Jerusalem to Jericho. He fell among brigands who stripped him, beat him and went off, leaving him nearly dead. Now a priest happened to pass by on that same road; he saw the man, and slipped by on the other side. In the same way, a Levite came to the spot, saw him, crossed to the other side of the road, and passed by. But a Samaritan on his journey came to the place. When he saw the man, he felt compassion for him – he bent over him and dressed his wounds, pouring oil and vinegar on them. Then he placed him on his mount, and took him to an inn where he looked after him. The next day, he gave the innkeeper two silver coins, and told him, 'Take good care of him, and whatever you spend in excess, I will repay when I come back.' So, in your opinion, which of the three has proved to be close to the man who fell into the hands of brigands?" The doctor of the Law replied, "The one who showed compassion towards him." Jesus told him, "Go, and do likewise."

Martha and Mary (LUKE 10:38–42)

As Jesus was on his way with his disciples, he came to a village where a woman named Martha welcomed him into her home. She had a sister called Mary who sat down at the Lord's feet and listened to him. Meanwhile Martha bustled about preparing the meal and she ended up by telling Jesus, "Lord, do you not mind that my sister is leaving me to do the serving all by myself? Tell her to help me." But the Lord answered, "Martha, Martha, you worry and fret about many things when only one is needed. Mary has chosen the better part; it will not be taken away from her."

The parable of the rich farmer (LUKE 12:15–21)

Jesus was once asked to intervene in a matter of inheritance. He said to the crowd which was around him, "Watch out!

Beware of any kind of covetousness, for human life does not depend on affluence." Then he told them this parable. "A rich man had fields which yielded such large crops that he wondered what to do, for he had not enough room to store them up. 'Oh! This is what I shall do,' he said to himself, 'I will tear down my barns and build larger ones where I shall store up all my grain and my other goods. Then I shall tell myself: You have got all you need for many years. Take things easy, eat, drink, and enjoy yourself.' But God said to him, 'You fool! This very night your life will be demanded of you, and what you have hoarded, whom will it profit?' This is what happens to those who store up wealth for themselves instead of becoming rich in God's sight."

The parable of the great banquet (LUKE 14:15–24)

One day during a meal, one of the guests told Jesus, "Blest is the one who will partake in the meal in God's kingdom!" He answered, "There was once a man who gave a great banquet to which he invited many people. In due time he sent his servant to tell the guests, 'Come, for all is ready.' But they all alike began to make excuses. The first one said, 'I have bought a piece of land. I must go and see it. Please excuse me.' Another one told him, 'I have bought five yoke of oxen, and I am on my way to try them out. I do apologize.' Still another one said, 'I have just got married; that is why I cannot come.'

"The servant went back and reported everything to his master who got very angry and said, 'Go quickly around the streets and lanes in the town and bring back the poor, the disabled, the blind, and the maimed.' The servant came back and said, 'Your orders have been carried out but there is still room.' Then the master told him, 'Go along the country roads and paths, and compel people to come, so that my house may be full. For, believe me, none of those who were invited will get the slightest taste of my banquet.' ''

The lost sheep and the lost coin (LUKE 15:1–10)

The tax collectors and sinners gathered round Jesus to listen to him. The Pharisees and the legal experts were indignant and mumbled, ''This man welcomes sinners and eats with them!'' So Jesus told them these two parables. ''Which of you, having a hundred sheep and losing one of them, does not leave the ninety-nine others in the wilderness to go and search for the one which is lost until he finds it? And having done this, he lays it on his shoulders, rejoicing. When he gets home, he calls together his friends and neighbours and tells them, 'Rejoice with me, for I have found my sheep which went astray.' This is how, I tell you, there will be more rejoicing in heaven for a single sinner who repents than for ninety-nine just who need not repent.

''Or, if a woman owns ten silver coins and loses one, will she not light a lamp, sweep her house, and search carefully until she finds it? And after this, she will call together her friends and neighbours and tell them, 'Rejoice with me, for I have found the silver coin that I had lost.' This is how, I tell you, there is jubilation in the presence of God's angels for a single sinner who repents.''

A father and his two sons (LUKE 15:11–32)

Jesus *continued with a third parable on the same theme*. ''There was once a man who had two sons. The younger one said to him, 'Father, give me right away the share of goods I shall inherit.' So the father divided his goods between his sons. A few days later, the younger son gathered up all his belongings and went to a far-off country where he squandered his goods in a dissolute life. When all his money was spent, the country where he was living experienced a severe famine and he started to be badly in need.

"So he hired himself out to one of the citizens of the country who sent him to his fields to feed the swine. He would gladly have eaten the pods that were fed to the swine, but nobody gave him anything. Then he came to his senses and said to himself, 'How many of my father's employees have more than enough to eat while I am here starving to death! I will go back to my father and tell him: Father, I have sinned against heaven and you. I am no longer worthy to be called your son. Treat me like one of your employees.' So he set off to go back to his father's place.

"While he was still some distance away, his father saw him, and was moved with compassion. He ran to his son, took him in his arms, and kissed him. And his son told him, 'Father, I have sinned against heaven and you. I am no longer worthy to be called your son.' But the father said to his servants, 'Hurry and bring the best clothes, and let him put them on. Let him wear a ring on his finger and sandals on his feet. Bring the fattened calf and slaughter it. We are going to celebrate and rejoice, for this son of mine was dead and he has come back to life, he had gone astray and is found.' And they started celebrating.

"The elder son was in the fields. On his way back, when he came near to the house he heard music and dancing. He called one of the servants and asked him what was going on. 'Your brother has come back,' the servant answered, 'and your father has slaughtered the fattened calf because he has returned safe and sound.' The elder son became angry and refused to go in. His father came out and entreated him but he replied, 'I have been labouring for you all these years and not once did you give me a kid for a celebration with my friends! And here comes this son of yours who has squandered your goods with loose women, and you have the fattened calf slaughtered!' But his father said to him, 'You my son have always been with me, and everything that is mine is yours. But it was important to celebrate and to rejoice since this brother of yours was dead, and is alive again; he went astray, and is found.' "

The grateful Samaritan (LUKE 17:11–19)

On his way to Jerusalem, Jesus passed through the borderland between Samaria and Galilee. As he entered a village, ten lepers came towards him. They stood at a distance – *for they were forbidden to enter into contact with anybody who was not suffering from leprosy*. They began to cry out, "Jesus! Master! Have compassion on us." When Jesus saw them, he said to them, "Go and show yourselves to the priests" – *for this was what every cured leper had to do*. As they went away, they were made clean. When one of them saw that he was healed, he came back, praising God at the top of his voice, and throwing himself at Jesus's feet, he thanked him. Now the man was a Samaritan. This made Jesus remark, "Were not the ten of them healed? Where are the other nine? This stranger is the only one to have come back to give glory to God." And he told the Samaritan, "Rise up, go! Your faith has saved you."

The Pharisee and the tax collector (LUKE 18:9–14)

For the benefit of those who are too self-assured and look down on other people, Jesus told this parable. "Two men, one a Pharisee and the other one a tax collector, went up to the Temple to pray. Standing apart on his own, the Pharisee prayed thus within himself, 'I thank you, O Lord, for not being like other people: grasping, unjust, adulterous, or like that tax collector. I fast twice a week, and give away ten per cent of my income.' The tax collector stood at some distance and dared not lift up his eyes to heaven. He beat his breast, saying, 'O God, have compassion on me, a sinner.' I tell you, this man went home reconciled with God, but the other one did not. For all who set themselves up will be humbled, but all who humble themselves will be raised up."

Jesus blesses little children (MARK 10:13–16)

People brought little children to Jesus for him to touch, but the disciples rebuked those who did so. Jesus became indignant with his disciples and told them, "Let the little children come to me, and do not stop them, for the kingdom of God belongs to those who are like them. In truth I tell you, whoever does not welcome the kingdom of God like a little child will not enter it." Then he took them in his arms and, laying his hands on them, he blessed them.

Jesus visits Zacchaeus (LUKE 19:1–10)

Jesus entered Jericho and went through the town. Now there was a rich man there named Zacchaeus, a senior tax collector. He was trying to see who Jesus was but, being too short, he could not manage because of the crowd. So he ran ahead and climbed up a sycamore tree to get a glimpse of Jesus who was to come that way. When Jesus reached the spot, he looked up and said, "Hurry, Zacchaeus, and come down, for today I must stay at your house." He came down at once and welcomed Jesus with joy. All who saw this started to grumble, "Now he is the guest of a sinner!" But Zacchaeus stood there and declared to the Lord, "Listen, Master, I am going to give half of my property to the poor, and if I have cheated people, I will repay them four times over." So Jesus said, "Today salvation has come to this house since he too is a son of Abraham. Indeed the Son of man has come to seek out and save those who have gone astray."

The healing of a blind man (MARK 10:46–52)

As Jesus was leaving Jericho surrounded by his disciples and a large crowd, there was a blind beggar called Bartimaeus, Timaeus's son, sitting at the side of the road. When he heard that it was Jesus of Nazareth who was passing by, he started to shout out, "Jesus, son of David, have compassion on me!" Many people rebuked him and ordered him to keep quiet, but he cried out all the more loudly, "Son of David, have compassion on me!" Jesus stopped and said, "Call him." So they called out to the blind man, telling him, "Take heart! Get up! He is calling you." Throwing off his cloak, he jumped to his feet and went to Jesus who asked him, "What do you want me to do for you?" The blind man answered, "Master, let me recover my sight." Jesus told him, "Go. Your faith has restored you to health." At that very moment, he recovered his sight and began to follow Jesus.

The good shepherd (JOHN 10:1–3, 9–18)

Once again, Jesus started teaching, "It is the very truth I am telling you. Whoever does not go into the sheepfold by the door, but breaks into it, is a thief and a bandit. But the one who enters by the door is the shepherd of the flock. The watchman lets him in, and the sheep hear his voice. One by one, he calls his own sheep and leads them out.

"I am the door of the sheepfold. Whoever goes in through me will be secure; they will go in and out, and find pasture. The thief comes only to steal, to kill and to destroy. But I have come so that they may have life and have it to the full.

"I am the good shepherd. The good shepherd offers his life for his sheep. But the hired man – since he is not the shepherd to whom the sheep belong – abandons the sheep as soon as he sees a wolf coming, and runs away. So the wolf catches hold of the sheep and scatters them. He runs away, for he is only a hired man and does not care about the sheep.

"I am the good shepherd – I know my sheep, and my sheep know me, just as the Father knows me and I know the Father, and I offer my life for my sheep.

"I have other sheep still, and they do not belong to this fold. I must lead them too. They will listen to my voice, and there will only be one flock, led by one shepherd.

"The Father loves me because I offer my life in order to take it up again. Nobody takes it from me, but I offer it of my own free will, for I have power to offer it and power to take it back. Such is the command I have received from my Father."

Jesus enters Jerusalem (MATTHEW 21:1–11)

When Jesus and the disciples reached Bethphage on the Mount of Olives, near Jerusalem, he sent two of them ahead, saying, "Go to the village ahead of you, and straight away you will find a donkey tied up, with her colt next to her. Untie them and bring them to me. If anyone says anything, just tell them, 'The Lord needs them, but he will send them back without delay.' " This occurred in order to fulfil the words of one of the prophets, "Tell Jerusalem: Look, your king is approaching, humble and mounted on a donkey, mounted on her colt, the foal of a beast of burden."

So the disciples went off and followed Jesus' instructions. They brought back the donkey and her colt, placed their cloaks on their backs, and Jesus sat on them. Then a large crowd laid their cloaks on the road, while other people cut branches to carpet his path. The crowd which went ahead of him and those who followed were all proclaiming, "Hosanna to the son of David! Blessed is he who comes in the name of the Lord! Hosanna in the highest heavens!" When Jesus entered Jerusalem, the whole city was in turmoil. "Who is this man?" people wondered. The crowds answered, "This is Jesus, the prophet from Nazareth in Galilee."

The Temple is cleansed by Jesus (JOHN 2:14–22)

In the Temple of Jerusalem, Jesus found people trading oxen, sheep and pigeons, as well as money-changers seated at their tables. So he made a whip out of cords, and he drove them all out of the Temple, with their sheep and their oxen. He swept away the money-changers' coins, and overturned their tables. And he said to those selling pigeons, "Get all this out of here, and stop making a trading centre out of my Father's house." Then the disciples remembered the words from the Scriptures, "Zeal for your house will devour me."

Then people came up and asked him, "What sign can you show us to justify your actions?" Jesus answered, "Pull down this Temple and in three days I shall raise it up again." The people replied, "It took forty-six years to build this Temple, and you could raise it up again in three days?" But he was speaking of the Temple that was his body. So when Jesus rose from the dead, his disciples remembered his words and they believed the Scriptures and what he had said *on that day.*

The parable of the two sons (MATTHEW 21:28–32)

Jesus asked chief priests and Jewish officials what they thought about this parable. "A man had two sons. He told one of them, 'Son, go and work today in my vineyard.' His son answered, 'I do not want to go.' But later on, he changed his mind and went. The man asked the same thing of his other son who answered, 'Yes, father', but did not go. Which of the two has done what his father asked?" They replied, "The first one." Then Jesus said to them, "I tell you the truth. Tax collectors and prostitutes are going ahead of you into God's kingdom. For John the Baptist came to show you the way of justice, but you did not believe him, whereas the tax collectors and the prostitutes did. And even when you became aware of this, you did not change your minds and believe him."

The parable of the wine growers (MATTHEW 21:33–46)

Jesus continued before the same audience: "Listen to another parable. A landowner planted a vineyard which he surrounded with a fence; he dug a winepress, and built a watch-tower. Then he rented the vineyard to wine growers and went abroad. At harvest time, he sent his servants to the wine growers in order to collect his share of the grapes. But they caught hold of the servants, beating one, killing another, and stoning a third. Again the landowner sent servants, in greater number than the first time, but they were treated in the same way. Finally he sent his son, thinking, 'At least they will respect my son.' But when the wine growers saw the son, they said to each other, 'Here is the heir. Come on, let us kill him and get hold of his inheritance.' Then they seized him, threw him out of the vineyard, and killed him. When the landowner comes back," Jesus asked, "what will he do to those wine growers?" They answered, "He will put those wretches to death and will rent his vineyard to other wine growers who will give him his share of the grapes at harvest time."

Then Jesus asked them, "Have you never read in the Scriptures, 'It is the very stone rejected by the builders which has become the head cornerstone. This is what the Lord has done, a marvel in our sight'? And so I tell you: the kingdom of God will be taken from you and given to a people who will make it bear fruit."

When they heard the parables, the chief priests and the Pharisees realized that they were aimed at them, but although they would have liked to arrest Jesus, they were afraid of the crowds who considered him to be a prophet.

The widow's offering (MARK 12:41–44)

Jesus sat down opposite the Temple treasury and watched the crowd putting money into it. Many rich people put in large sums. There came a poor widow and she put in two very small coins. Then he called his disciples and said to them, "I tell you the truth. This widow has put in more than all the others; for they contributed out of what they could spare, whereas in her poverty she has given all she had to live on."

The ten bridesmaids (MATTHEW 25:1–13)

Jesus went on to say, "This will make you understand how to wait for the kingdom of heaven: ten bridesmaids went with their lamps to meet the bridegroom. Five of the bridesmaids were foolish and the other five were wise for they had taken oil with them, whereas the former had not. Since the bridegroom was late, they all felt drowsy and eventually fell asleep. But at midnight a voice cried out, 'Here he comes. Go and meet him.' So all the bridesmaids woke up and trimmed their lamps. The foolish ones said to the wise, 'Give us some of your oil, for our lamps are going out.' But they replied, 'There may not be enough oil for us and for you. You should rather go to the traders and buy some for yourselves.' They had gone off when the bridegroom arrived. Those who were ready went into the wedding hall with him and the door was closed. When the other bridesmaids arrived at last, they began to cry out, 'Lord, Lord, open to us.' But he replied, 'In all truth, I do not know you.' So keep watch, for you do not know either the day or the hour."

The last judgement (MATTHEW 25:31–45)

Jesus also spoke about the end of the world. "When the Son of man comes in his glory, and all his angels with him, he will be seated on his throne of honour. Before him will be gathered all human beings of all ages and he will separate people as a shepherd separates sheep from goats. He will place the sheep on his right and the goats on his left.

"Then the king will tell those on his right hand, 'Come, O blessed of my Father, and inherit the kingdom prepared for you since the foundation of the world. For I was hungry and you gave me food, I was thirsty and you quenched my thirst, I was an alien and you welcomed me, I was naked and you clothed me, I was sick and you visited me, I was a prisoner and you came to see me.' Then the just will ask him, 'When was it, Lord, that we saw you hungry and gave you food, that you were thirsty and we quenched your thirst? And when did we see you as an alien and welcomed you, or naked and clothed you? When did we find you sick or in prison and visited you?' And the king will answer, 'I tell you the truth. In so far as you did it to one of the least of these brothers and sisters of mine, it was to me that you did it.'

"Then he will tell those on his left, 'Go far away from me, for I was hungry and you gave me nothing to eat, I was thirsty and you gave me nothing to drink, I was an alien and you did not welcome me, I was naked and you did not clothe me, I was sick and in prison and you did not come and see me.' Then they too will ask, 'When was it, Lord, that we have seen you hungry or thirsty, or an alien, or naked, sick or in prison, and we did not assist you?' The king will answer, 'I tell you the truth. Just as you did not do it to one of the least of these, you did not do it to me.' "

The Eucharist

Jesus is anointed at Bethany (MARK 14:1–9)

The Feast of the Passover and of Unleavened Bread was to take place in two days' time. The chief priests and the law experts were looking for a scheme which would allow them to arrest Jesus and put him to death, for they said, "We cannot do it during the Feast or there might be a riot among the people."

While Jesus sat at table in the house of Simon the leper at Bethany, a woman came in with an alabaster jar filled with very expensive perfume, pure nard. She broke the jar, and poured the ointment over Jesus' head. Some people became indignant and said, "Why did she waste this perfume? We could have sold it for a lot of money to give to the poor." And they started to scold the woman.

But Jesus told them, "Leave her alone. Why are you harassing her? She has done a beautiful deed for me. Poor people will always be with you, and whenever you wish to do so, you can show kindness to them. But you will not always have me. She has done what she could – she has anointed my body beforehand for its burial. In truth I tell you, wherever the joyful news *of the Gospel* is announced in the whole world, what she has done will be told in memory of her."

Judas conspires with the priests (MARK 14:10–11)

Then Judas Iscariot, one of the Twelve, went to the chief priests and offered to hand Jesus over to them. They were delighted at the offer and promised to give him money. So from that moment, he looked for an opportunity to betray Jesus.

The preparation of the Passover meal (MARK 14:12–16)

On the first day of the Feast, when it was the custom to sacrifice the Passover lamb, the disciples asked Jesus, "Where do you want us to go and prepare your Passover meal?" So he sent two of them, telling them, "Go into the city, and you will meet a man carrying a jug of water. Follow him, and say to the landlord of the house that he enters, 'The master asks you to show us the room where he will eat the Passover meal with his disciples.' He will show you a large room upstairs, all furnished and ready. Prepare the meal for us there." The disciples set off and went into the city where they found everything as he had told them. And they prepared the Passover meal.

Jesus washes his disciples' feet (JOHN 13:1–17)

That very evening, Jesus knew that his time had come to leave this world and to go to the Father. Having loved his own in this world, he showed them how utterly he loved them.

While Jesus and his disciples were at table, the devil had already persuaded Judas Iscariot to betray his master. As for Jesus, knowing that the Father had committed all things into his hands, and that he had come from God and was going back to him, he got up from the table, removed his tunic, and girded himself with a towel. He poured water into a basin and began to wash his disciples' feet, and to wipe them with the towel he was girded with.

He came to Simon Peter who exclaimed, "Lord, are you going to wash my feet?"

Jesus answered, "What I am doing, you cannot grasp it now, but later on you will understand."

"You will never wash my feet!"

"If I do not wash you, you will have nothing in common with me."

"Then, Lord, do not wash my feet only, but also my hands and my head."

"Whoever has taken a bath has no need to wash, except for the feet, for all the rest is clean. And you are clean, though not every one of you."

Indeed he knew who was going to betray him, and that was why he said not every one was clean.

After giving them this sign and putting on his tunic again, Jesus returned to his place and said, "Do you understand what I have done to you? You call me Master and Lord, and rightly so, for this is what I am. So if I, your master and lord, have washed your feet, you too must wash one another's feet. I have given you an example so that you act as I have done to you. In truth I tell you, there are no servants greater than their master, nor messengers greater than the one who sent them. If you grasp these things, blest are you if you put them into practice."

The institution of the Eucharist (MARK 14:22–25)

While they were eating, Jesus took bread, blessed it, broke it and gave it to his disciples, saying, "Take it. This is my body." Then he took a cup, and having given thanks, he handed it to them and all drank from it. He told them, "This is my blood, the blood of the covenant shed for many. I tell you the truth: never again shall I drink wine until the day when I drink it new in the kingdom of God."

A new command (JOHN 13:33-35)

After Judas Iscariot had gone out, Jesus said, "Little children, I shall only be with you for a little longer. You will look for me, but as I said to the people – and I am now saying it to you – where I am going, you cannot come. I give you a new command, that you love one another. You must love one another just as I have loved you. It is by the love you have for one another that everyone will know you as my disciples."

The prayer for the unity of Christians (JOHN 17:1A,11B,20-21)

After Jesus had spoken these words, he lifted up his eyes to heaven and said, "Father, I am coming to you. Keep faithful to your name those you have given me, so that they may be one as you and I are one.

"I do not pray only for these who are here but also for those who will believe in me through their message. May they all be one: just as you, Father, are in me and I in you, may they be also in us, so that the world may believe that it was you who sent me."

The Passion

Jesus in Gethsemane (MARK 14:26–42)

After singing the psalms, Jesus and his disciples went to the Mount of Olives. On the way, Jesus said, "You will all desert me, for it is written in the Scriptures, 'I will strike the shepherd, and the sheep will be scattered.' But after my resurrection, I shall go ahead of you to Galilee." Peter told him, "Even if all of them desert you, I will not." Jesus answered him, "I assure you in all truth that this very night, before the cock crows twice, you will have denied me three times." But Peter replied vehemently, "Even if I have to die with you, I will not deny you." And all the others said the same.

They came to a place called Gethsemane. Jesus said to his disciples, "Remain here while I am praying." He took with him Peter, James and John. Terror and anguish took hold of him. He said to them, "My soul is grieved to the point of death. Wait here, and stay awake." Going a little farther, he fell to the ground and prayed that, if it were possible, this hour might pass him by. He said, "Abba, Father! For you everything is possible: remove this cup of sorrow from me. However, let it not be my will but yours which is done." He went back to his disciples and found them asleep. He said to Peter, "Simon, are you sleeping? Could you not stay awake for one hour? Stay awake and pray not to undergo trial, for the human spirit is well inclined but its nature is weak." Again he went and prayed, saying the same words. Again he came back and found them asleep, so hard was it for them to keep their eyes open.

They could find nothing to say to him. A third time he came and told them, "Are you still resting and sleeping? That will do. Now is the hour when the Son of man is betrayed into the hands of sinners. Come on! Get up! See, my betrayer has come."

Jesus is arrested (MARK 14:43–52)

And at once, while Jesus was still speaking, Judas, one of the Twelve, appeared; and with him there was a crowd armed with swords and clubs, sent by the chief priests, the legal experts and the elders of the people. Now the betrayer had agreed upon a signal with them: "The one I kiss is the man you want. Take hold of him and lead him away under guard." When Judas arrived, he immediately went up to Jesus and said, "Master", and kissed him. The others took hold of him and arrested him. One of the bystanders drew his sword and struck the high priest's servant, cutting off his ear.

Then Jesus spoke. "Am I a bandit that you have come to take me with swords and clubs? I was among you day after day teaching in the Temple and you never laid a hand on me. But let the Scriptures be fulfilled." Then all his disciples deserted him and ran away. A young man following Jesus was wearing nothing but a linen cloth. They caught hold of him, but he let go of the cloth and ran off naked.

Jesus is condemned by the High Council of the Jews (MARK 14:53–65)

They took Jesus to the high priest; all the chief priests, the elders of the people and the legal experts were gathered there. Peter had followed him at a distance, right to the high priest's courtyard. There, seated with the guards, he warmed himself at the fire.

The chief priests and all the High Council were looking for evidence against Jesus so as to have him put to death, but they did not manage to find any. Indeed, several people did bring false accusations against him, but their evidence did not agree. Then some got up and bore this false evidence against him, saying "We heard him say, 'I will destroy this Temple made by human hands, and in three days I will build another one that will not be made with hands.'" Yet even on this point their evidence did not agree. Then the high priest stood up before the whole assembly and asked Jesus, "Have you got nothing to answer? What is this evidence they are bringing against you?" But Jesus kept silent and made no answer. The high priest put a second question to him, saying "Are you the Christ, the Son of the Blessed One?" Jesus answered, "I am. And you will see the Son of man seated at the right hand of the Almighty One and coming with the clouds of heaven." Then the high priest tore his robes and said, "What need do we have of other witnesses? You have heard his blasphemy. What is your verdict?" All condemned him as deserving death.

Some of them started to spit at his face and to beat him, saying, "Prophesy!" And the guards struck him as well.

Peter denies Jesus (MARK 14:66–72)

Peter was still down below in the courtyard. One of the high priest's maids came up and saw Peter warming himself. She looked hard at him and said, "You too were with Jesus, the man from Nazareth." But he denied it, saying, "I do not know or understand what you mean." And he went away under the porch. A cock crowed. When the maid saw what Peter had done, she again said to the bystanders, "This man is one of them." But once more he denied it. A little later it was the guards' turn to tell him, "You are certainly one of them. Besides, you are Galilean." But Peter cursed and said, "I swear that I do not know the man you are speaking of." At once the cock crowed a second time and Peter remembered Jesus's words, "Before the cock crows twice, you will have denied me three times." He burst into tears.

Jesus before Pilate (MARK 15:1–15)

First thing in the morning, the chief priests conferred with the people's elders, the doctors of the Law and the other members of the High Council. *The Jews were not allowed to condemn someone to death. That right belonged exclusively to the Romans.* They had Jesus bound and they took him to hand him over to Pilate, the Roman governor.

Pilate asked him, "Are you the king of the Jews?" He answered, "You are saying so." The chief priests accused him of many things, but he answered nothing. Pilate asked, "Have you nothing to reply? See all that they are accusing you of!" But to Pilate's amazement, Jesus made no reply at all.

For the Feast of the Jews, Pilate was in the habit of releasing a prisoner of their choosing. Now, among the rebels in prison condemned for murder during an uprising, there was a man called Barabbas. When the crowd came up and asked for the customary pardon, Pilate asked them, "Do you want me to release for you the king of the Jews?" For he was well aware that it was out of envy that the chief priests had delivered him up. But they prompted the crowd to demand Barabbas's release instead. So Pilate spoke up again, "Then what shall I do with the man whom you call the king of the Jews?" They shouted back, "Crucify him!" Pilate asked them, "What wrong has he done?" But they shouted even louder, "Crucify him!"

So Pilate, anxious to satisfy the crowd, released Barabbas for them, and after having Jesus flogged, he delivered him to be crucified.

Jesus is crowned with thorns (MARK 15:16–20)

The soldiers led him inside the palace, that is, the Praetorium, and summoned the whole cohort. They dressed him up in a purple cloak and they twisted some thorns into a crown which they set on his head. And they began to salute him, "Hail, King of the Jews!" They struck him on the head with a reed, spat on him and knelt before him to pay him homage. When they were tired of making fun of him, they took off the cloak, dressed him with his own clothes, and led him outside to crucify him.

The crucifixion (MARK 15:21–24A)

Normally a person condemned to be crucified would carry the horizontal beam of the cross which would serve for the crucifixion. Jesus carried the beam a short distance, but was unable to go further because of the treatment he had received. That is why the soldiers compelled a passer-by coming back from the fields, Simon of Cyrene, father of Alexander and Rufus, to carry the cross. They brought Jesus to the place called Golgotha (which means "place of the skull"). They offered him wine mixed with myrrh, but he did not drink it. And then they crucified him.

Jesus forgives (LUKE 23:34)

Jesus said, "Father, forgive them, for they do not know what they are doing." As for the soldiers, they cast lots to divide his clothes among them.

Jesus and his mother (JOHN 19:25–27)

Near the cross of Jesus, there stood his mother and his mother's sister, Mary the wife of Clopas, and Mary Magdalene. When Jesus saw his mother and *the apostle John*, the disciple whom he loved, beside her, he said to his mother, "Woman, here is your son." Then he said to the disciple, "Here is your mother." And from that moment, the disciple took her into his home.

Jesus on the cross is mocked (MARK 15:25–32A)

It was around nine in the morning when they crucified him. The inscription of the charge against him read, "The King of the Jews." Two criminals were crucified with him, one on his right and the other on his left. The passers-by mocked at him, shaking their heads and saying, "Aha! You were to destroy the Temple and rebuild it in three days! So save yourself and come down from the cross!" The chief priests and the doctors of the Law laughed at him among themselves in the same way. "He has saved other people," they said, "and he cannot save himself, this Messiah, King of Israel! Let him now come down from the cross, that we may witness it and believe in him!"

The two criminals (LUKE 23:39–43)

One of the criminals abused him also, saying "Are you not the Christ? Save yourself, and us too!" But the other one rebuked him, "Don't you have the slightest respect for God? You have been sentenced to the same punishment as him, but justly so in our case, for we are paying for what we have done. As for him, he has done nothing wrong." Then he said, "Jesus, remember me when you come into your kingdom." Jesus answered him, "It is true: this very day you will be with me in paradise."

The death of Jesus (MARK 15:33–39)

From noon until three there was darkness over the whole land. At three, Jesus cried out in a loud voice, "Eloi, Eloi, lama sabachthani?" which means "My God, my God, why have you forsaken me?" When they heard him, some of the bystanders said, "Listen, he is calling Elijah!" One of them ran and soaked a sponge in vinegar; he put it on the end of a reed and gave it to him to drink, saying, "Wait! Let us see if Elijah will come and take him down."

Then, with a loud cry, Jesus breathed his last.

The curtain of the Temple was torn in two from top to bottom. And when the centurion who stood in front of Jesus saw how he had died, he said, "Truly this man was the Son of God!"

The burial of Jesus (MARK 15:42–47)

The evening came. Since it was the day before the sabbath the day for its preparation, Joseph of Arimathaea, a respected member of the High Council, who was also himself waiting expectantly for the Kingdom of God, summoned up his courage and went to ask Pilate for the body of Jesus, *for it would not be possible to bury him on the sabbath day.* Pilate wondered if Jesus was really dead: he summoned the centurion, and when he was told that it was the case, he granted the body to Joseph. So Joseph bought a shroud, took Jesus down from the cross, wrapped him in the shroud and laid him in a tomb which had been carved out of the rock. Then he rolled a stone to close the tomb entrance. Mary Magdalene and Mary the mother of Joses took note of the place where he was laid.

The Resurrection

The empty tomb (JOHN 20:1–10)

Very early on the first day of the week, while it was still dark, Mary Magdalene went to the tomb. She saw that the stone at the entrance of the tomb had been removed. So she ran to Simon Peter and the other disciple – *John* – whom Jesus loved. She told them, "They have taken the Lord out of the tomb, and we do not know where they have laid him."

So Peter set off with the other disciple to go to the tomb. They were both running, but the other disciple was faster than Peter and was the first to reach the tomb. He bent forward and saw the linen wrappings on the ground, but he did not go in. Following him, Simon Peter arrived and went into the tomb; he saw the linen wrappings on the ground and the cloth that had covered Jesus's head, not lying with the other cloths but rolled up by itself. Then the other disciple who had reached the tomb first, went in also. He saw and he believed. Indeed, until then the disciples had not yet understood that according to the Scriptures, Jesus was to rise from the dead. Then the two disciples went home.

Jesus appears to Mary Magdalene (JOHN 20:11–18)

But Mary Magdalene stood outside, near by the tomb, weeping. While she sobbed, she bent down to look inside the tomb; and she saw two angels clothed in white, sitting one at the head and the other at the feet of the place where the body of Jesus had been lying. They said to her, "Woman, why all this weeping?" She answered them, "Because they have taken away my Lord, and I do not know where they have laid him." While she was speaking, she turned round and saw Jesus standing there, but without knowing that it was him. He said "Woman, why are you weeping? Who are you looking for?" Thinking he was the gardener, she said to him, "If you have taken him away, tell me where you have laid him, and I shall go and fetch him." Jesus said, "Mary!" She turned round and said to him in Hebrew, "Rabbouni!" – which means Master. Jesus told her, "Do not cling to me, for I have not yet gone to the Father. But go to my brothers and tell them that I am going up to my Father and your Father, to my God and your God." So Mary Magdalene went and announced to the disciples, "I have seen the Lord", and she told them what he had said to her.

The disciples on the way to Emmaus (LUKE 24:13–35)

Now, on that same day, two disciples were going to a village called Emmaus, some seven miles from Jerusalem. They were talking together about all that had happened. As they discussed, Jesus himself caught up with them and started to walk by their side; but their eyes were kept from recognizing him. He asked them, "What are you discussing, with such a downcast air about you?" The one named Cleopas answered him, "You must be the only person in Jerusalem not to know what has happened there during the last few days!" He asked them, "What is this all about?"

They answered him, "It is about Jesus of Nazareth, a prophet mighty in action and speech before God and the whole people. Our chief priests and leaders handed him over to be sentenced to death, and they had him crucified. As for us, we were hoping he would be the one to set Israel free. But that is not all. Two full days have gone by since all this happened, and now some women from our group have stunned us. They went to the tomb early this morning and did not find the body! They even came back telling us that they had had a vision of angels who declared he was alive. Some of us went to the tomb and found it exactly as the women had said, but they did not see him at all."

Then he said to them, "You foolish people, so slow in believing all that the prophets have announced! Was it not necessary that the Christ should suffer before entering into his glory?" Then he started with Moses and went through all the prophets, explaining to them all that was said about himself in the Scriptures.

When they got near the village to which they were going, Jesus acted as if he would go on his way. But they urged him to stay with them, saying, "Evening is coming, and the day is nearly over." So he went in and stayed with them. When he was at table with them, he took bread, blessed it and broke it, and gave it to them. Their eyes were opened and they recognized him. But he vanished from their sight. They said to each other, "Were not our hearts burning within us while he was talking to us on the road and explaining the Scriptures to us?" At once they set off to return to Jerusalem. There they found the Eleven gathered with their companions who said to them, "The Lord has risen indeed and has appeared to Simon Peter!" Then the two coming from Emmaus told them what had happened on the way and how they had recognized him when he broke the bread.

Jesus appears to his disciples (JOHN 20:19–29)

On the evening of that first day of the week, when the disciples had locked themselves in a house because they were afraid, Jesus appeared, stood in their midst and said, "Peace be with you!" Then he showed them his hands and his side. When the disciples saw the Lord, they were overcome with joy; and Jesus said to them again, "Peace be with you! As the Father has sent me, so am I sending you." After saying this he breathed on them and said, "Receive the Holy Spirit. Whenever you forgive someone's sins, they are truly forgiven *by God*."

One of the Twelve, Thomas, called the Twin, was not there when Jesus came. The other disciples told him, "We have seen the Lord." But he answered them, "Unless I see the nail marks in his hands and put my finger on them, and unless I place my hand in his side" – *for Jesus's side had been pierced on the cross* – "I will not believe."

Eight days later the disciples were again locked in the house, but this time Thomas was with them. Jesus appeared, stood in their midst and said, "Peace be with you!" Then he spoke to Thomas, "Put your finger here, there are my hands. Stretch out your hand and put it in my side. Do not doubt but believe." Thomas exclaimed, "My Lord and my God!" Jesus told him, "You believe because you see me. Blest are those who have not seen and yet believe."

Jesus appears in Galilee (JOHN 21:1–14)

A few days later, by the Lake of Tiberias, Jesus appeared again to his disciples. This is how it happened. Simon Peter, Thomas called the Twin, Nathanael from Cana in Galilee, Zebedee's sons and two other disciples were there together. Simon Peter told them, "I am going out to fish." They replied, "We are coming with you." So they went and got into the boat, but they caught nothing that night.

Early in the morning, Jesus stood on the beach, but the disciples did not know it was him. Jesus asked them, "Children, have you caught any fish?" They answered him, "No." He told them, "Cast your net on the right side of the boat and you will find some." They did so and they found they were unable to haul the net in, so abundant was the catch. *John*, the disciple whom Jesus loved, said to Peter, "It is the Lord." When Simon Peter heard this, he dressed (for he had taken off his clothes to work) and jumped into the water. The other disciples came back in the boat, towing the net full of fish. They were only some hundred yards from the shore.

Once they were ashore, they saw some bread and also fish cooking over a charcoal fire. Jesus told them, "Bring some of the fish you have just caught." So Simon Peter climbed back into the boat and hauled the net ashore. It was filled with one hundred and fifty-three large fish, but in spite of the number, it had not burst. Jesus said, "Come and have breakfast." None of the disciples dared ask him, "Who are you?" for they knew it was the Lord. Jesus came, took the bread and gave it to them, and did the same with the fish. This was the third time that Jesus appeared to his disciples after rising from the dead.

Peter's new start (JOHN 21:15–19)

Once breakfast was over, Jesus asked Simon Peter,

"Simon son of John, do you love me even more than these others do?"

He answered, "Yes, Lord, you know that I love you."

Jesus told him, "Feed my lambs."

He asked him a second time, "Simon son of John, do you love me?"

He answered, "Yes, Lord, you know I love you."

Jesus told him, "Take care of my sheep."

Then he asked him a third time, "Simon son of John, do you love me?"

Peter was hurt that Jesus asked him a third time if he loved him; he said, "Lord, you know everything. So you know that I love you."

Jesus told him, "Feed my sheep. I tell you the truth: when you were young, you dressed by yourself and went wherever you wished. But once you are old, you will stretch out your arms and someone else will dress you and lead you where you would rather not go."

With these words, Jesus suggested through which kind of death Peter would glorify God.

Then he told him, "Follow me."

The Acts
of the Apostles

The Acts of the Apostles

The Ascension (ACTS 1:3–11)

After his Passion, Jesus appeared to his apostles, and during forty days he gave them many proofs that he was alive, speaking to them about the kingdom of God. One day, at table with them, he ordered them not to leave Jerusalem but to wait there for what the Father had promised. "It is", he told them, "what you have heard me speak of: John the Baptist baptized with water, but in a few days' time you will be baptized with the Holy Spirit."

When they were meeting together, they asked Jesus, "Lord, is it now that you will restore the kingship in Israel?" He answered them, "It is not for you to know the times or seasons that the Father has decided by his own authority. But when the Holy Spirit comes upon you, you will receive new energy to be my witnesses not only in Jerusalem, but throughout Judea and Samaria and to the ends of the earth."

Having said this, he ascended before their very eyes, and a cloud took him out of their sight. As they were gazing towards heaven while Jesus went away, two men dressed in white appeared and said to them, "Men of Galilee, why are you standing there gazing into the sky? This Jesus who has been taken from you will come back in the same way as you have seen him go to heaven."

The gift of the Holy Spirit (ACTS 2:1–17,32,36–38,41–42)

On Pentecost day, they were all together in one place. Suddenly
there was the sound of a mighty wind blowing from the sky,
and it filled the house where they were. Then there appeared
tongues of fire – like flames – which separated and came to
rest on each one of them. They were all filled with the Holy
Spirit and started to speak in other languages as the Spirit made
each one of them able.

Now there were devout people from every nation under
the sun staying in Jerusalem. At the sound of the wind, they
all assembled, bewildered to hear their different languages. They
were amazed and marvelled, "These people who are speaking,
are they not all Galileans? How is it then that each of us hears
them speak in our own mother tongue? Parthians, Medes and
Elamites, inhabitants of Mesopotamia, Judea and Cappadocia,
Pontus and Asia, Phrygia and Pamphylia, Egypt and the lands
of Libia near Cyrene, both Jews and proselytes from Rome,
Cretans and Arabs – all of us hear them proclaim God's marvels
in our own tongues!" Everyone was amazed and puzzled, asking
one another what all this meant, whereas others made fun of
it, saying, "They have got drunk with new wine."

Then Peter stood up with the Eleven and spoke to them
in a loud voice, "Citizens of Judea and all of you who are
staying in Jerusalem, listen carefully to my words and know
that these people are not drunk as you imagine. Besides, it
is only nine in the morning. No, this is what was announced
by the prophet Joel, 'In the last days, the Lord declares, I shall
pour out my Spirit on all living beings: your sons and your
daughters will prophesy, your young people will see visions
and your old people will have dreams.' " Then he spoke to
them about Jesus whom God had raised from the dead, "and

we are all witnesses to this fact", he told them. Then he added, "Let all the people of Israel be well convinced of this: the Lord and Christ whom God has established is none other than this Jesus whom you crucified."

When they heard these words, they were cut to the heart and they asked Peter and the other apostles, "Brothers, what are we to do?" Peter answered them, "Turn your hearts towards God, and let each one of you be baptized in the name of Jesus the Christ for the forgiveness of your sins. Then you will receive the gift of the Holy Spirit." They accepted what they had been told and were baptized. On that day, about three thousand were added to the disciples' number. They all remained faithful to the apostles' teaching, to fraternal fellowship, to the breaking of bread and to the prayers.

The healing of a crippled beggar (ACTS 3:1–12,15–17,19)

One day, Peter and John were going to the Temple for the prayer at three in the afternoon. A man crippled from birth was being carried to the gate called Beautiful, as he was every day, so that he could beg from those going into the Temple. When he saw Peter and John about to enter, he asked them for alms. Peter and John gazed at him, and Peter told him, "Look at us." The man did not take his eyes off them, expecting them to give him something. Then Peter said to him, "I have neither silver nor gold, but I am going to give you what I have: in the name of Jesus the Christ from Nazareth, walk!" He took him by the right hand and helped him up. At once the man's feet and ankles became strong, and leaping up, he stood and began to walk; he entered the Temple with them, leaping and jumping and praising God.

Everybody saw him walking and praising God, and they

recognized him as the man who used to sit begging at the Beautiful Gate. They were amazed and marvelled at what had happened to him. The man clung to Peter and John, and everybody ran up to them at Solomon's Portico in great excitement. When Peter saw the crowd, he addressed them, "People of Israel, why are you amazed by what has happened, and why do you stare at us as if it were through our own power or due to our holiness that we have made this man walk? It is faith in the name of Jesus which has given the strength to this man whom you see and who is well known to you. The faith received from Jesus has brought this man back to health in the presence of all of you. Whereas you killed Jesus, the prince of life, God has raised him from the dead. But you and your leaders – now I know, brothers and sisters – had no idea of what you were doing. So change your hearts and turn towards God so that your sins be forgiven."

The first Christian community (ACTS 4:32–37)

With great power, the apostles continued to bear witness to the resurrection of the Lord Jesus, and the people showed them great respect.

The whole community of believers was united in heart and mind. Nobody claimed private ownership of any possessions, for everything was held in common. So no one was in need, because those who owned lands or houses sold them; then they brought the proceeds of what was sold to the apostles who distributed it to those in need.

It was in this way that Joseph, a Levite from Cyprus, to whom the apostles gave the name Barnabas, which means Man of Consolation, sold the field he owned, brought the money and laid it at the apostles' feet.

The death of Stephen (ACTS 6:2–13;7:1,51–60)

The disciples were increasing in number. The Twelve called a full meeting of the disciples and told them, "It would not be right for us to neglect the word of God in order to serve at meals. So, friends, you will choose from among you seven men of good reputation, filled with the Holy Spirit and with wisdom, and we shall entrust them with this duty. As for us, we shall continue to devote ourselves to prayer and to the service of the word of God."

The assembly was unanimous in agreeing with this proposal. They elected Stephen, a man filled with faith and the Holy Spirit, Philip, Prochorus, Nicanor, Timon, Parmenas and a proselyte from Antioch called Nicolas. They were presented to the apostles who prayed and laid their hands on them. The word of God continued to spread. The number of the disciples increased rapidly in Jerusalem and a great many of the priests adhered to the faith.

Filled with grace and power, Stephen worked wonders and great signs among the people. Then certain people from Cyrene and Alexandria – members of the synagogue known as the Freedmen's – as well as others from Cilicia and Asia, started to argue with Stephen; but they could not stand up to him because of his wisdom and the Spirit which inspired his speech. So they bribed some people to say, "We have heard him use blasphemy in speaking of Moses and of God." Then they stirred up the people as well as their leaders and the doctors of the Law. They took Stephen by surprise and led him before the High Council. There they produced false witnesses who said, "This man never stops saying things against the holy Temple and the Law."

The high priest asked him, "Is this true?" Stephen answered,

"Brothers and fathers, listen to me!" – *Then he spoke to them at length, reminding them how often God had addressed his people and how often they had disobeyed him. Finally he said to them,* "You are forever resisting the Holy Spirit, just as your ancestors always did! Could you name one single prophet your forefathers did not persecute? They killed those who foretold the coming of the Righteous One, and now you have become his betrayers, his murderers, you who received the Law through angels but have not kept it." Those words provoked them to great fury and anger against Stephen.

But filled with the Holy Spirit, Stephen gazed into heaven where he saw the glory of God, and Jesus standing at his right hand. He exclaimed, "Now I can see heaven wide open, and the Son of man standing at God's right hand." All the High Council members began to shout out and they stopped their ears. They all rushed together against him, dragged him out of the city and began to stone him. The witnesses laid their clothes at the feet of a young man named Saul. While they were stoning him, Stephen prayed, "Lord Jesus, receive my spirit." Then he fell on his knees and cried out, "Lord, do not hold this sin against them." With these words he fell asleep. And Saul approved of their killing him.

The Ethiopian treasurer (ACTS 8:26–40)

Like Stephen, Philip was one of the seven chosen to help the apostles.
The angel of the Lord spoke to him, "Go towards the south, along the desert road which leads from Jerusalem to Gaza." Philip set off. Now an Ethiopian eunuch was returning home after being on pilgrimage to Jerusalem. He was chief treasurer at the queen of Ethiopia's court. Sitting in his chariot, he was reading the book of the prophet Isaiah. The Spirit said to Philip,

"Run up to this chariot." When Philip caught up with it, he heard the Ethiopian senior officer reading Isaiah and asked him, "Do you understand what you are reading?" He answered, "How could I, unless someone explains it to me?" So he invited Philip to come up and sit at his side. Now he was reading this passage, "Like a lamb led to the slaughter, like a sheep dumb before its shearer, so he did not open his mouth. In his humiliation, he was denied justice. Who will ever speak of his descendants, since his life on earth has been cut short?" The eunuch turned towards Philip and asked him, "Tell me. Is the prophet speaking about himself or about someone else?"

Then Philip, starting with this passage from the Scriptures, explained to him the joyful news of the coming of Jesus. On their way, they came to a watering place, and the eunuch said, "Now that we have water, is there any obstacle to my being baptized?" Philip answered, "There is none, if you believe with all your heart." The eunuch declared, "I believe that Jesus the Christ is the Son of God." He ordered his chariot to stop. Both of them went down into the water and Philip baptized the eunuch.

When they came out of the water, Philip was taken away by the Spirit of the Lord. The eunuch saw him no more, but carried on his way rejoicing. As for Philip, he found himself at Azotus and, travelling on, he proclaimed the good news in all the towns as far as Caeserea.

Saul's conversion (ACTS 8:1,3;9:1–20)

At that time a violent persecution broke out against the Christian community in Jerusalem. Everyone except the apostles was scattered throughout the rural districts of Judea and Samaria. Saul began to wreak havoc upon the community, going from house to house, arresting both men and women and sending them to prison.

Breathing threats and slaughter against the Lord's disciples, he went to the high priest and asked him for letters of introduction to the synagogues in Damascus. He was seeking to be commissioned to arrest any followers of the Christ whom he might find there, men and women alike, and bring them bound to Jerusalem.

On his way, as he approached Damascus, he was suddenly surrounded with an intense light from heaven. He fell to the ground. A voice said to him, "Saul, Saul, why are you persecuting me?" He asked, "Who are you, Lord?" The answer came, "I am Jesus, the very one you are persecuting. But rise up and go to the town. There you will be told what you have to do." Saul's companions stood there speechless, utterly amazed: they could hear the voice but could not see anyone. Saul got up, but when he opened his eyes, he could see nothing at all. So he had to be taken by the hand to Damascus. During three days, he was blind and could neither eat nor drink.

In Damascus there was a disciple named Ananias. In a vision the Lord called him by his name. "Here I am, Lord," he answered. The Lord told him, "Go to the Straight Street, and at the house of Judas you will ask for Saul from Tarsus. At this moment, he is praying, and he has seen in a vision a man named Ananias coming to lay his hands on him so that he may recover his sight." Ananias answered, "Lord, many people have spoken to me about this man and all the harm he has done to your disciples in Jerusalem. He has come here, commissioned by the chief priests, to arrest everyone who calls upon your name." But the Lord replied, "Go, for I have chosen this man to be my instrument in making my name known to the Gentiles and their rulers, and to the people of Israel. And I myself will show him all he will have to suffer for my name's sake."

So Ananias went to the house of Judas where he laid his hands on Saul, saying, "Brother Saul, I have been sent by the Lord Jesus who appeared to you on the road as you were coming here. You will recover your sight and be filled with the Holy Spirit." Something like scales fell from Saul's eyes and at once he recovered his sight. He was baptized immediately, and once he had taken some food, he regained his strength.

Saul, *who later on was to be called Paul*, spent only a few days with the disciples in Damascus, and without delay he began to preach in the synagogues, "Jesus is the Son of God."

St Paul's Letters

Apostolate

2 *Corinthians* 5:14–15,17–20

Christ's love overwhelms us when we realize that if one person died for all, then all have passed through death. And he died for all, so that the living live no longer for themselves but for him who died and rose again for their sake. For all who are in Christ, there is a new creation: the old being has vanished, a new creature has appeared.

All of this is God's work – through the Christ, he has reconciled us to himself and has entrusted us with the task of enabling others to enjoy the same reconciliation. In other words, God was in the Christ, reconciling the world to himself, not taking anyone's faults into account, but entrusting us with the message of reconciliation.

So on the Christ's behalf, we are sent to you on a mission; as though through our message it is God himself who is urging you, in the Christ's name, to let yourself be reconciled to him.

2 *Corinthians* 3:2–6,17–18

You yourselves are our letter, written on your hearts, to be read and understood by everyone. It is clear that you are a letter from Christ, entrusted to our care, written not with ink but with the Spirit of the living God, not on stone tablets but on the tablets of human hearts.

It is through Christ that we are confident in God's presence. There is no competence that we can claim as coming from

us. No, all our competence is from God, who has enabled us
to become servants of a new covenant, founded not on a
written code that takes life away, but in the Spirit who gives
life. For where the Lord's Spirit is, there lies freedom.

So with unveiled faces reflecting like mirrors the glory of
the Lord, all of us together are being transformed into the same
image that we reflect, becoming ever more radiant. This is
the work of the Lord who is Spirit.

2 Corinthians 4:7–11

We, the apostles, carry the treasure of the good news in jars
of clay. Thus it is clear that whatever happens to be
extraordinary is not from us but from God. We are subjected
to all kind of ordeals, but never are we crushed; we see no
way out, but never do we despair; we are hunted down, but
never caught; brought down but not destroyed.

Always and everywhere we bear the agony of Jesus in our
body, so that his life too may be visible in this same body.
For as long as we are alive, we are constantly given over to
death for Jesus's sake, so that his life too may be visible in our
mortal flesh.

Colossians 1:24–29

I rejoice now to be suffering for your sake, and in my body
to be completing all the ordeals Christ must still undergo for
the sake of his body, that is, the Church. I have been
commissioned by God to be its servant so as to make his message
fully known among you. Indeed, this was a mystery which
remained hidden throughout the ages, but which today has
been revealed to God's faithful people. It has pleased God to

make known to them how rich is the glory of this mystery among the Gentiles: it is Christ in you (*present among you*), the hope of glory. Such is the Christ we are proclaiming, urging and instructing everyone in all wisdom so that each one may be made perfect in him. That is the reason for all the trouble I take on your behalf, fighting with his energy which is mightily at work within me.

Message

1 Corinthians 15:1–6,8–10,14–15,17,19–22

Brothers and sisters, I want to refresh your memory in regard to the gospel message I preached to you; you received it and you remain loyal to it. It is through this message that you are being saved, if you hold firmly to it – unless you have believed in vain.

I passed on to you a tradition of prime importance that I myself had received: in accordance with the Scriptures, Christ died for our sins; he was buried; the third day, again in accordance with the Scriptures, he was raised and appeared to Cephas – *that is, Peter* – and later on to the Twelve, and then to more than five hundred brothers and sisters at one time, most of whom are still among us, while a few have fallen asleep. Last of all, as to a child born out of time, he appeared to me, the least of the apostles, unworthy of the title, since I persecuted God's Church.

But what I am now, I owe it to God's grace which was not given to me in vain; for I have worked harder than all the others – not I, however, but God's grace within me.

Now, if Christ did not rise again, our message is meaningless, and the same applies to your faith. We could even be blamed for misrepresenting God if we testified that he raised Christ when he did not. If Christ is not risen, your faith does not make sense, neither have you been freed from your sins. If it is only for this life that we have placed our hope in Christ, then we are the most pitiable of all human creatures.

In fact, however, Christ has been raised from the dead, the

first fruits of those who have fallen asleep. Just as death came through a human being, *Adam*, so through a human being *Jesus Christ*, has come the resurrection of the dead. If all human beings die because of the nature they share with Adam, in Christ all will be brought to life.

Galatians 4:4–6

At the proper time, God sent his Son, born of a woman and subject to the Law, in order to redeem the subjects of the Law, so that we may become God's children. As evidence that we are his children, God has sent the Spirit of his Son into our hearts, crying, "Abba! Father!"

Romans 7:14–15,22–25a; 8:1–4

We are well aware of the spiritual nature of the Law; but my nature is of flesh, enslaved by sin. I do not understand my own behaviour; for I do not do what I intend to do but the very things I hate.

In my heart of hearts, I delight in God's Law, but in my members I see another law which is at war with the law of my inner being, so that I become captive to the law of sin which dwells inside me.

What a wretched man I am! Who will rescue me from this body destined for death? It is God – thanks be to him! – through Jesus Christ our Lord.

Now, there is no longer any condemnation for those who are in Christ Jesus, for the Law of the Spirit, the giver of life in Christ Jesus, has set us free from the law of sin and death.

God has worked out what the Law, imposed from outside upon weak human nature, could not achieve: because of sin, he sent his Son in a human nature identical to any sinner's, so that he might wipe out sin from human nature. This was so in order that the Law's requirements might be fully met in us who no longer walk in the way of self-indulgence but of the Spirit.

Romans 8: 26-30

In our weakness the Spirit comes to our help, for we do not know how we ought to pray; so he intercedes within us with sighs that no words can express. And God, who sounds the human heart, knows the longing of the Spirit, and the Spirit's intercession for the faithful is always in keeping with the mind of God.

For we know that God makes everything work towards the good of those who love him and have been called according to his purpose. Indeed, those he knew in advance, he also predestined to reproduce the image of his Son, so that he might be the eldest of a vast number of brothers and sisters. And those who were thus predestined, he called; those who were called, he justified; those whom he justified, he made them share in his glory.

1 Thessalonians 4:13-14,16-18

Brothers and sisters, as regards those who have fallen asleep, we want you to be well assured, and not to let yourselves be carried away by grief like people who are without hope.

We believe that Jesus died and rose again. God enables those who have fallen asleep in Jesus to take part in his glory. Indeed, at the signal given by an archangel's voice, the Lord himself will come from heaven: all those who have died in Christ will be the first to be raised; then we who are still alive shall join them to go and meet the Lord. In this way we shall be with him for ever.

Therefore, comfort one another with such thoughts.

Faith

Romans 4:20–22

No disbelief made Abraham waver as regards God's promise.
On the contrary, fully convinced that God is able to perform
whatever he has promised, he drew strength from his faith and
gave glory to God. Such was Abraham's faith, and it was
credited to him as righteousness.

Philippians 3:4–14

As for me, I should have every reason to put my confidence
in my former values; and if anyone believes they have good
reasons for placing their trust in those values, I have far better
ones for doing so: circumcised eight days after my birth, I was
born an Israelite, of the tribe of Benjamin, a Hebrew born
of Hebrews; as far as the Law is concerned, a Pharisee; as for
religious fervour, a persecutor of the Church; as for
righteousness through observance of the Law, I was blameless.

But what I used to consider as assets, I now consider as
drawbacks because of Christ. And, before the supreme
advantage of knowing Christ Jesus my Lord, I hold all things
without exception as disadvantages.

For Christ's sake, I have accepted the loss of all things. I
consider everything as rubbish in order to gain him and to
be found in him, not as the outcome of some kind of
righteousness of my own, obtained through the observance
of the Law; it is due to faith in Christ – the righteousness that

comes from God and is based on faith. May I know Christ and the power of his resurrection, and take part in his sufferings by becoming like him in his death, and so, somehow, attain to the glory of God's risen children!

Not that I have already obtained this glory or that I am already perfect. No, I continue to seek it so that it may become my own, just as Christ has made me his own. No, brothers and sisters, I do not consider that I have made it my own; but this is what I do – I forget all that is past and thrust myself forward to run towards the goal, so as to win the prize that God invites us to receive in Christ Jesus: *the life of eternal communion with him.*

Galatians *2:20*

If I go on living, it is no longer I, but Christ who lives in me: subject to the limitations of human nature, my life is lived by faith in the Son of God who loved me and gave himself for me.

Galatians *3:26–28*

Through faith, you are all God's children in Christ Jesus; for every one of you who has been baptized into Christ has been clothed with Christ as with a new garment. From now on, it no longer matters whether you are Jew or Greek, slave or free, male or female: for all of you are one in Christ Jesus.

Love

Romans 12:9–18

Let your love be genuine. Avoid what is evil, cling to what is good. Love one another with mutual affection, regarding others as superior to yourselves. In the service of the Lord, do not be half-hearted, but work with conscientiousness and zeal. May your hope make you joyful. May hardship find you patient. Persevere in prayer, share with your brothers and sisters in need, practise hospitality willingly.

Call God's blessing on those who persecute you. Bless, never curse.

Be joyful when others are rejoicing; weep with those in sorrow. Show the same consideration for everyone: pay no regard to social status, but meet the humble on an equal footing. Do not be conceited about your own wisdom. Never return evil for evil. Look for what is good in everyone's sight and, if it is at all possible and as far as it depends on you, be at peace with everyone.

1 Corinthians 13

I may know every language, both of heaven and earth, yet if I speak without love, I am a resounding gong or a clashing cymbal. I may have the gift of prophecy to go deeper into every mystery and to grasp all fields of knowledge, and I may have faith enough to move mountains, yet if I am without love, I am nothing. I may give away all I have to the poor and even give up my body to be burned, yet if I have no love, it will do me no good.

Love is patient; love is kind; love is never jealous or boastful or arrogant or rude. It never seeks its own advantage, nor takes offence, nor harbours grudges. Love takes no pleasure in evil deeds, but finds its joy in the truth. It always makes allowances, always trusts, always hopes, always endures.

Love is endless. Prophecies? They will be swept away. Tongues? They will be silenced. Knowledge? It will be discarded. Why? Because our knowledge and our prophecies are imperfect; so when perfection appears, all imperfection will disappear.

When I was a child, I spoke like a child, thought like a child and reasoned like a child. When I grew up, I put an end to childishness. In the same way, what we see now is unclear, like a reflection in a bad mirror; but then we shall see face to face. Now my knowledge is imperfect; but then I shall know perfectly, just as God knows me.

Today faith, hope and love remain, all three; but the greatest of these is love.

Philippians 2:1–11

If you find the slightest encouragement in Christ, the slightest incentive in Love, the slightest communion in the Spirit, the slightest tenderness or compassion, then I urge you to make my joy complete by being of a single mind, one in love, one in feelings and thoughts. Do nothing out of selfishness or vain glory, but in full humility regard others as better than yourselves, and, instead of thinking only of your own interests, have regard for the interests of others.

Have among you the same mind as was in Christ Jesus:

He, being of the same status as God,
did not contemplate taking advantage
of his equality with God.

On the contrary, he humbled himself,
adopting the status of a servant,
and becoming as human beings are.

A human being in every respect,
he humbled himself even more,
obedient to the point of death,
death on a cross.

That is why
God has raised him high
and conferred on him the name
which is higher than all other names,

so that at the name of Jesus
every being in the universe
should kneel down

and everyone proclaim,
"Jesus Christ is Lord,
to the glory of God the Father."

Colossians 3:12–17

As God's chosen ones, members of his beloved people, clothe yourselves with tender compassion, kindness, humility, gentleness and patience. Accept one another, and when there arises a quarrel among you, forgive one another. The Lord has forgiven you; so it is now up to you to do the same. But above all, make love the bond of perfect harmony. And let

Christ's peace rule in your hearts, for it is to this peace that you have been called to form a single body. Always be thankful.

Let Christ's Word in all its fullness dwell in you. In all wisdom, teach and advise one another. With grace in your hearts, sing to God psalms, hymns and chants inspired by the Spirit. Let whatever you do in word or action be done in the name of the Lord Jesus, through whom you give thanks to God the Father!

Freedom

Galatians 5:1,13–16,22–6:2

By setting us free, Christ intends us to remain free. So stand fast, and do not let yourselves be placed again under the yoke of slavery.

Yes, brothers and sisters, you were called by God to be free, but do not use your freedom as an opportunity for self-indulgence. On the contrary, through love, become servants of one another, for the whole Law is summed up in a single command, "Love the other person just like yourself." But if you snap at one another, tearing each other to pieces, beware! You will end up by destroying each other.

That is why I tell you: let yourselves be guided by the Spirit, and you will no longer be tossed about by your instincts.

The fruit produced by the Spirit is love, joy, peace, patience, kindness, goodness, trustfulness, gentleness and self-control.

All who belong to Christ Jesus have crucified the passions and desires in themselves. And since we are living by the Spirit, let us be guided by the Spirit instead of seeking vainglory. Let there be no provocation and no envying among us.

Brothers and sisters, if one of you is caught in a misdeed, you who are inspired by the Spirit should set that person right in a spirit of gentleness, aware that you might be put to the test in the same way. Bear one another's burdens and so fulfil the law of Christ.

Unity

Romans 12:1–8

I urge you, brothers and sisters, considering God's mercies towards you, to offer to God your persons as a living, holy and pleasing sacrifice. This is the way to worship for you who are endowed with reason. Do not take the present world as a model, but let yourselves be transfigured through the renewal of your way of thinking, so that you may discern God's will – what is good, acceptable and perfect.

Through the grace granted to me by God, I urge each of you not to think of yourself more highly than you ought to, but to pass a balanced judgement on yourself, founded on the measure of faith which was assigned to you by God. Just as each of us has a body with various members that exercise diverse functions, all of us – though there are many of us – make up a single body in Christ, and we are all members of one another.

Our gifts differ according to the grace given to us, so let us use them wisely: if it is prophecy, in proportion to our faith; if it is service, in devoting ourselves to serving; if it is teaching, by teaching; if it is encouragement, by encouraging. When you give, do it generously, from your heart of hearts; if you are entrusted with some responsibility, carry it out conscientiously; if you practise compassion, let it be done with joy.

Ephesians 4:1–7,11–13,15–16

I, a prisoner for the Lord's sake, urge you to lead a life worthy of the calling to which you have been called. Being humble, gentle and patient, support one another in love, while passionately maintaining the unity of the Spirit through the peace which binds you together. Just as there is only one hope to which you are called, there is only one body, one Spirit, one Lord, one faith and one baptism, one God and Father of all who is above all, present in the midst of all, acting through all.

To each of us God's grace has been granted as Christ has allocated it, assigning some to be apostles, others to be prophets, or to preach the Gospel, or to be pastors and teachers. This is how Christ co-ordinates his holy people for its ministry, and how the Body of Christ is being built up. And the day will come when we shall all attain unity in the faith and in the full knowledge of the Son of God, and all together we shall make up this Person, fully mature, to the measure of Christ's fullness.

Then, witnessing in love to the truth, we shall grow up in every respect until we are identified with Christ, the head, by whom the whole body is fitted and held together. For each of its joints contributes by its own strength, and each of its parts works according to its function, so that the body grows until it has built itself up wholly in love.

Prayer

Philippians 1:3-6,9-11

Every time I think of you, I express my gratitude to God, and each time I pray for you, I do it with joy, for I remember the part you have played in the preaching of the Gospel, from the very first day until now. I am fully confident that God, who started this fine work in you, will go on completing it for the day of Jesus Christ's coming.

And when I pray for you, I ask that your love for one another may abound ever more, together with full knowledge and complete understanding, for these will help you to discern what is best. And so you will be innocent and blameless for the day of Christ's coming, filled through him with the fruit of righteousness, to the glory and praise of God.

Philippians 4:4-7

Always rejoice in the Lord. Again I say: be joyful! Let your kindness be evident to everyone. The Lord is near. So do not worry about anything, but in everything, with prayer and supplication, address your requests to God and give him thanks. Then the peace of God which is far beyond our understanding will keep your hearts and your thoughts rooted in Christ Jesus.

Ephesians 3:14-21

On my knees before the Father, from whom every parenthood in heaven and on earth draws its name, I pray that, out of the riches of his glory, he may strengthen your inner being through the power of his Spirit. And I pray also that, through faith, Christ may dwell in your hearts. Then, rooted and built up in love, you will have the strength, with all God's holy people, to grasp and measure all the dimensions of Christ's love, which is beyond all knowledge. And so you will be filled with the total fullness of God.

Glory be to him whose power at work in our hearts is able to achieve far more than we may ever ask or conceive! Glory be to him from one generation to the next in the Church and in Christ Jesus for ever and ever. Amen.

Suffering

Philippians 1:20–27

It is my eager expectation and hope that in no way shall I be put to shame, but be bold enough, now as always, so that Christ be honoured in my body, be it by my life or my death.

For, to me, life means Christ Jesus, and therefore it would be a positive gain for me to die. On the other hand, if I can still be of some use while living in the body, I do not know what to choose and I am caught in this dilemma: on one hand, I wish to go and be with Christ, for that is what I am longing for; and yet, for your sake, it is more necessary to remain in this body. So, after all, of this much I am certain: I shall stay and continue with you, in order to promote your progress and joy in the faith. In that way, when I am back among you, you will have abundant reasons to be proud in Christ Jesus on my account.

Only, may you always behave in a manner worthy of Christ's Gospel. And so I shall know, whether I come and see you or hear of you from afar, that you are standing firm in one spirit, unanimous in striving for the faith of the Gospel.

2 Timothy 2:3–13

As a good soldier of Christ Jesus, endure your share of hardship. No soldier gets involved in civilian affairs if he wants to please his enlisting officer. In the same way, when an athlete wins a contest, he will receive his award only if he has competed according to the rules. Or again, it is the farmer who excels in his work who ought to receive the first share of the crops. Think over what I am saying, for the Lord will make you understand everything.

Remember the Gospel that I am preaching, "Jesus Christ, raised from the dead, a descendant of David." It is on account of this Gospel that I am suffering, chained up like a criminal. But God's message cannot be put in chains. This is why I endure everything for the sake of those whom he has chosen, so that they too may obtain the salvation that in Christ Jesus goes hand in hand with eternal glory. You can fully rely on the saying:

> If we have died with him,
> with him we shall also live.
> If we stand firm,
> with him we shall reign.
> If we are unfaithful,
> he remains faithful,
> for he cannot deny himself.

Romans 8:31–39

If God is for us, who can be opposed to us? If he did not spare his own Son, but gave him up for our sake, can we not expect that, with Christ, he will also shower on us all his gifts? Who can bring any accusation against those whom God has chosen? Since it is God who justifies, who can condemn? Did not Christ Jesus die for our sake and, even more, raised from the dead, is he not interceding for us at God's right hand?

Is there anything which can cut us off from the love which

Christ has for us – whether ordeals, distress or persecution; lack of food or clothes; peril or violence? For it is written in the Scriptures,

> For your sake, O Lord,
> every day we are in peril of our life,
> like sheep to be slaughtered.

No, in all these things, the victory that was beyond our means has been won thanks to him who loves us. For I am certain of this: neither death nor life, neither angels nor demons, neither what exists nor what is to come, neither powers, nor heights, nor depths, nor any creature whatsoever, no, nothing will be able to come between us and the love which God has shown to us in Christ Jesus our Lord.

The Other Letters

The Letter to the Hebrews

Hebrews 11:1,8–10,13–16

This is what faith is about: through faith we already possess what we are hoping for, and we let ourselves be convinced of the reality of what we do not see.

It was by faith that Abraham obeyed God's calling and set out for a place he was to receive as an inheritance. And he set out without knowing where he was going. By faith he dwelt in the promised land as if he were a foreigner: he lived in tents with Isaac and Jacob, heirs with him of the same promise, for he was looking forward to the city with strong foundations, designed and built by God.

The patriarchs were living by faith when they died before the fulfilment of what had been promised to them. But they saw it from a distance and they rejoiced in it, acknowledging that they were only nomads and foreigners on earth. People who see themselves in this way clearly show that they are searching for their real country. Now, if they had had in mind the country where they had come from, they could have found a way to return to it. No, they were longing for a better country, their heavenly one. This is why God is not ashamed to be called their God.

Hebrews 12:1–3

Surrounded as we are by such a huge cloud of witnesses, let us too cast aside everything we are burdened with and the sin

which clings to us, so as to run with perseverance the race
which is set before us. Let us fix our gaze on Jesus who leads
us in our faith and brings it to perfection: to win the joy
prepared for him, he endured the cross without paying attention
to its shame, and took his seat at the right hand of God's throne.
Ponder the way in which he persevered in the face of such
hostility from sinners, and then you will not lose heart nor
grow weary.

St James's Letter

James 1:2–3,12–18

My brothers and sisters, count it as a source of true joy whenever you are submitted to any kind of trial, for as you know, the testing of your faith produces tenacity.

And blest is the person who shows tenacity when trials occur; having stood the test, that person will inherit the crown of life promised by the Lord to those who love him. Let no one say in the hour of temptation, "It is God who is tempting me", for God cannot be tempted by evil, nor does he tempt anyone. But we are tempted by the appeal and seduction of our own craving. Then craving conceives and gives birth to sin which eventually brings forth death.

Do not be deceived, my beloved. From God come only excellent gifts, good in all respects, for he is the Father of all light; and no alteration nor any shadow due to change is to be found in him.

By his will of love, he gave us new birth through the message of truth, so that from now on we might be the first fruits of his whole creation.

James 1:19–25

Beloved brothers and sisters, let everyone be prompt to listen but slow to speak and to get angry, for human anger never produces God's righteousness. So get rid of all that is not clear within you and all remnants of malice, and with meekness welcome the Word which has been planted in you and which is able to save your lives.

However, you must put the Word into practice, and not merely be hearers who deceive themselves. For when we content ourselves with hearing the Word without putting it into practice, we are like those who look at their features in a mirror, and after looking at them, they go off and forget them immediately. But when we keep our gaze fixed on the perfect law, the law of freedom, and keep to it – not by hearing it and forgetting it immediately afterwards, but by putting it into practice – we shall be blest for having done so.

James 2:1–5,8

Brothers and sisters, let no class prejudice enter into your faith in Christ Jesus, our Lord in glory.

Now suppose a man comes into your place of worship, handsomely dressed with a gold ring at his finger, and at the same time a poor man comes in, in shabby clothes. If you take notice of the handsome man, and tell him, "Please, come and sit here", while you say to the poor man, "Stand in that corner", or "Squat down there", are you not making distinctions among people which reveal your poor judgement?

Listen, my beloved brothers and sisters. Has not God chosen the poor in the world's sight to make them rich in faith and to make them inherit the kingdom he has promised to those who love him? To act rightly, you should fulfil the supreme law of the Scriptures, "Love the other person just like yourself."

James 2:14–17

Brothers and sisters, what use is it for someone who has never done any worthwhile deed to say, "I have faith"? Is this faith going to save that person? Suppose some of the brothers or sisters are in need of clothes or are without their daily food. If one of you says to them, "My very best wishes. Keep warm and eat plenty", without giving them what they lack, what good is that? It is the same for faith: if it does not go together with worthwhile deeds, it is well and truly dead.

St Peter's Letters

1 Peter 1:3-4,6-9

Blessed be God, the Father of Christ Jesus our Lord! In his great mercy, he has given us a new birth into a living hope through the resurrection of Christ Jesus from the dead, and into an incorruptible inheritance, undefiled and unfading, which is kept for us in heaven.

In this you find great joy, even though you may still have to suffer all kinds of trials for a while, so that the sincerity of your faith – more valuable than perishable gold, which is none the less tested by fire – may be proved, to your praise and honour, when Jesus Christ appears.

This Christ, you have not seen him and yet you love him. Still without seeing him you believe in him and are filled with a radiant joy that cannot be described; for you are sure of obtaining the outcome of your faith – which is salvation.

1 Peter 2:20-25

What is there remarkable about enduring a punishment for wrongdoing? But it is commendable in God's sight if you endure suffering patiently while fulfilling your duty. This is what you have been called to do since Christ suffered for you, leaving you an example so that you should follow in his steps.

He had done nothing wrong, never uttered any deceit. When he was insulted, he did not retaliate; when he was overwhelmed with pain, he threatened nobody. Instead, he left the matter in the hands of God, the upright judge. He bore our sins in his own body on the wood of the cross, so that we might die to our sins and live for righteousness. It is by his wounds that you have been healed, you who were going astray like sheep, but now have returned to the one who looks after your lives and watches over them like a shepherd.

1 Peter 3: 8–9,13–16a

All of you, in unity of heart and mind, love one another like brothers and sisters, with compassion and humility. Do not return evil for evil or insult for insult. Instead, respond with a blessing for that is what you have been called to in order to obtain God's blessing.

Who is going to harm you if you are determined to do only what is good? Furthermore, blest are you if you suffer for doing what is right. Let no one frighten or trouble you. It is the Lord Christ you must take into account, keeping him holy in your hearts. Always be ready to answer anyone who asks you the reason for the hope that is in you. However, do it with courtesy, respect, and a conscience which is at peace.

2 Peter 1:16–21

We were not following cleverly devised myths when we made known to you the power of our Lord Jesus Christ's coming. No, we have witnessed his glory with our own eyes. Indeed, he received honour and glory from God the Father when a voice coming from the transcendent glory declared, "This is my Son in whom is all my love. In him my heart rejoices." We ourselves heard this voice come from heaven while we were with Christ on the holy mountain of his transfiguration.

So the message of the prophets is confirmed, and you will do well to pay attention to it. It is indeed like a lamp which lights up the dark place where you are, until the day breaks and the morning star rises in your hearts.

It is of the utmost importance that you should understand this: prophecies from the Scriptures are never a matter for personal interpretation, since none of them is the result of human initiative. No, it is under the Holy Spirit's impulse that some people have spoken on God's behalf.

St John's Letters

1 John 1:1–3

What was at the beginning of all, what we have heard, what we have seen with our own eyes, what we have gazed on and touched with our hands, is the Word of life.

Indeed this life made itself visible. We saw it and we bear witness to it, in proclaiming to you the eternal life which was with the Father and was manifested to us.

What we have seen and heard, we proclaim it to you, so that you too may share what was given to us – our communion with the Father and with his Son, Jesus Christ.

1 John 3:1–2

Try to imagine how great is the love the Father has showered on us, that we should be called children of God! And that is what we are. If the world does not know us, it is because it does not know God.

Beloved, we are already God's children, but what we shall be in the future has not yet been revealed. What we know is that when he appears we shall be like him, for we shall see him as he is.

1 John 3:16–24

Jesus laid down his life for us – this is how we know what love is about. In turn, we ought to lay down our lives for one another. When someone well off sees a brother or sister in need and yet refuses to help, how could God's love abide in this person? Children, our love must not be just words and mere talk, it must be active and consistent with truth. In this way we shall be certain of belonging to the truth, and in God's presence we shall reassure our hearts whenever they condemn us, for God is greater than our hearts, and he knows everything.

Beloved, if our hearts do not condemn us, we may have full confidence in God's presence: whatever we ask from him, we receive it, because we keep his commands and do what pleases him. And this is his command: that we should believe in the name of his Son, Jesus Christ, and love one another just as he commanded us. All who keep his commands abide in God, and God abides in them. And this is the proof that he abides in us – the Spirit he has given us.

1 John 4:7–13,17–21

Beloved, let us love one another, since love comes from God. Whoever loves is born of God, and knows him. Whoever refuses to love does not know him, since God is love. This is how God's love was made manifest among us: God sent his only Son into the world, so that we might have life through him. Here is how this love is revealed: it is not we who loved God, it is God who loved us by sending his Son for the forgiveness of our sins.

Beloved, if God loved us so much, we too should love one another. No one has ever seen God, but in so far as we love one another, God abides in us, and his love becomes perfect in us. This is the proof that we abide in him, and he in us – he has granted us to have a share in his Spirit.

Love becomes perfect among us when we can draw near

without fear to the Day of judgement, because already in this world we have become as Jesus is. There is no room for fear in love; indeed, perfect love banishes fear, for fear is linked up with punishment. And, for whoever lives in fear, love has not yet come to fulfilment.

As for us, we love, because he loved us first. People who say, "I love God", and hate their brothers or sisters do not speak the truth. If they do not love a brother or a sister they see, they cannot love God they do not see. Such is the command we have received from him: whoever loves God, must also love their brother and sister.

1 John 5:2–5

We know that we love God's children when we love God and put his commands into practice; for it is when we keep them that we love God. Besides, these commands are not burdensome, for whoever is born of God overcomes the world. What has given us victory? Our faith. For who can overcome the world but the person who believes that Jesus is the Son of God?

Psalms

Psalms

Psalm 8

How great is your name, O Lord our God,
throughout all the world!

Set high over all the earth,
majestic to the highest heavens,
you fashion the praise of babes,
you silence the boasts of your foes.

When I see the moon and the stars,
the sky which you have formed,
what are human beings, that you remember them,
and their children, that you care for them?

Scarcely less than angels you made them;
you crowned them with glory and honour;
all things created are theirs,
to take care of them in your name.

Both sheep and cattle you gave them,
and even the wild beasts,
birds flying, the fish of the sea,
with all that dwells in the deep.

How great is your name, O Lord our God,
throughout all the world!

Psalm 23

The Lord is my shepherd,
so nothing I shall lack;
he leads me across green pastures,
and there I find rest;
he brings me to quiet waters
where he quenches my thirst.

He guides me along safe paths,
on account of his love.
Though I walk through the valley of darkness,
I shall fear no harm;
you are close with your rod and staff,
to comfort my soul.

You spread before me a banquet,
keeping my enemy away;
you perfume my head with oil,
my cup overflows.

Your goodness and kindness will pursue me
every day of my life;
in the house of the Lord I shall live
through the ages to come.

Verses from Psalm 31

I take shelter in you, O Lord,
I shall never be put to shame;
you are just, make haste to save me,
incline your ear to my prayer.

Be a rock to protect me,
a fortress to keep me safe;
Lord, you are my fortress and rock,
so guide me on account of your love.

Keep me safe from the traps they have laid,
for in you I trust;
into your hands I commend my spirit,
for you have made me yours, O Lord.

God of truth, far from you
all those who serve false gods;
but I shall rejoice and be glad
on account of your constant love.

Lord, you saw my distress,
you beheld the trouble of my soul;
you saved me from my enemies' hands,
you put me back on my feet and set me free.

Have compassion on me, O Lord,
for distress is upon me;
my eyes are consumed with tears,
wasting my body and my soul.

For see, I am weary with grief,
my life goes to waste in tears;
my strength has faded away
and my bones are destroyed.

My enemies treat me with contempt,
    all my neighbours mock;
my friends shudder at my sight,
    in the streets they flee.

I am banished from living mind,
    as though I were dead,
rejected and thrown aside
    like a thing of no use.

I hear the muttering of crowds,
    terror on every side!
They are plotting together against me
    to take away my life.

But always I trust in you, O Lord,
I repeat to myself, "You are my God",
every moment of my life lies in your hand,
    save me from the hands of my foes.

Look kindly on your servant, O Lord,
    save me by your love;
let me not be ashamed when I pray,
    shame on wicked–doers.

How wonderful is your goodness, O Lord,
    the goodness you show your friends;
you are good for all who believe in you
    in the face of all humankind.

In your presence, you keep them hidden,
        safe from intrigues;
    you conceal them all in your tent,
        far from the cursing of tongues.

Yet once I thought in my grief,
    "He has lost me from sight",
but I called out, pleading for your help,
        and you heard my cry.

So love the Lord, all his saints!
He takes care of all his friends.
Be brave and be of good heart,
    all who hope in the Lord!

Psalms 42–43

        Like a deer that yearns
            for a cooling stream,
        so is my soul athirst
            for you, my God.

My soul is thirsting for God,
        for the living God;
    when shall I come and see
        the face of God?

        Tears are my only food
            by day and by night;
    all day long I hear them say,
        "Where is your God?"

Once I went with the throng
to the House of God,
amidst shouts of rejoicing and praise
on the lips of the crowd.

Why do you agonize, my soul?
Why faint in my breast?
Hope in God: I shall praise him still,
my Saviour, my God.

When my heart is about to break,
I turn my thoughts,
from Jordan and Hermon's land,
to you, the lowly hill.

The deep summoning the deep
in the roaring of the flood,
the might of your raging waves
overwhelms my soul.

If by day the Lord is pleased
to reveal his love,
his song in my heart by night
prays the God of my life.

I implore my defender, my God,
"Why did you forget me?
Why must I now go in grief,
oppressed by the foe?"

All my bones are crushed with shame
at the insults I endure;
always I hear them say,
"Where is your God?"

Why do you agonize, my soul?
Why faint in my breast?
Hope in God: I shall praise him still,
my Saviour, my God.

Give sentence in my favour, O God,
against the godless;
from the power of the wicked and the false
deliver my soul.

For you are my defender, O God,
why cast me aside?
And why must I endure such pain
at the hands of my foes?

Send out your light and your truth,
let them be my guides;
bring me back to your holy hill,
to the house where you dwell.

I shall go to the altar of God,
he is the source of joy;
I shall play on the harp, I shall sing
to praise him, my God.

Why do you agonize, my soul?
Why faint in my breast?
Hope in God: I shall praise him still,
my Saviour, my God.

Verses from Psalm 90

Lord, you have been our refuge,
    from age to age!

Before the mountains came forth,
or the face of the earth was made,
    from age to age you are God.

You turn us back to the dust,
saying, "Return now, children of mortals!"
In your sight, a thousand years are a day,
a day past, like a watch of the night.

They are swept away like a dream,
like the morning grass in the fields:
at dawn it springs up and blooms,
by evening, it is withered and dry.

So teach us to number our days,
that in wisdom our hearts may grow;
how long still, O Lord? Come soon,
show compassion on all who serve you.

Fill us each morning with your love,
all our days, with your joy and praise;
for the times of distress, give joy,
for the years when sadness was our lot.

Let your servants look upon your deeds,
and show your glory to their children;
your kindness, O Lord, be upon us,
you confirm the work of our hands.

Psalm 103

Give praise to the Lord, O my soul,
all my being, praise his holy name,
give praise to the Lord, O my soul,
never forget all he fills you with.

The Lord forgives all your misdeeds,
he heals you of every kind of ill,
he rescues your life from the grave,
and crowns you with his love and tenderness;
he comes to fill you with every kind of good,
and like the eagle's, your youth is renewed.

For the Lord works out salvation,
he brings justice for all the oppressed.
He revealed to Moses his ways,
to the children of Israel his great deeds.

The Lord is compassion and love,
rich in patience, abounding in concern;
he does not hound us with reproaches,
he does not weigh us down with the past;
he does not treat us according to our sins,
nor repay us as our ways would deserve.

As high as the sky above the earth,
great is his love for all who love him,
as the east is far from the west,
so far he removes all our sins.

As a father is gentle to his child,
so good is the Lord to all who love him;
he knows in what manner we were made,
he remembers that we rose from the dust.

As for mortals, their days are like grass,
they blossom like flowers in the fields:
one breath of the wind, they are no more,
and their places will not see them again.

But the Lord's love for all who adore him
is eternal, unending in days;
to their children's children he is faithful,
if they keep his covenant and laws,
and take care to fulfil his commands.

The Lord has set his throne in the heavens,
and over all is his kingdom with its strength;
give praise to the Lord, all his angel-servants
who fulfil his commands,
attentive to the sound of his word.

Now bless the Lord, all his saints,
faithful servants, eager to fulfil his will;
give praise to the Lord, all his works,
in every place where his majesty is known;
and give praise to the Lord, O my soul.

Psalm 116

I love the Lord, for he hears
the sound of my prayer;
he gives heed to me in his love
whenever I implore him.

The snares of death were all round me,
all the horror of the grave;
plunged in anguish, without any hope,
yet I called on the Lord's name.

For the Lord is compassionate and good,
yes, our God is tenderness;
The Lord, he defends the poor,
when I was weak, he saved my life.

Return then, my soul, to your rest,
for you know how good is the Lord.
He has saved my soul from death,
and my feet from stumbling.
I shall walk in the presence of God,
in the land of the living.

I believed, even when I said,
"Too intense is my pain!"
And in my grief, I have said,
"To hope in mortals is vain!"

Then what can I offer to the Lord
for his generosity to me?
I shall lift high the cup of salvation,
I shall praise his holy name.

I shall fulfil my vows to God,
with his servants looking on.
Very costly in the Lord's sight
is the death of every friend.

For me, your servant from my birth,
you have severed my bonds.
I shall offer a sacrifice to praise,
I shall call on the name of the Lord.

I shall fulfil my vows to God,
with his servants looking on,
in the courts of the House of the Lord,
in your midst, O Jerusalem!

Psalm 130

Out of the very depths of the abyss,
I cry to you, O Lord;
Lord, hear my cry, and listen carefully
to the sound of my calling.

If you remember, O Lord, all our faults,
who then can survive?
But with you our forgiveness is sure,
and so we adore you.

My soul is eager for the Lord,
I trust his every word;
my soul is more eager for the Lord
than a watchman for the dawning.

With the Lord there is tenderness and love,
his compassion overflows;
so Israel will be redeemed by the Lord
from all its sins.

Prayers

Prayers by Brother Roger

Jesus Christ, inner Light, enable us to welcome your love, that we may experience a joy. We love you, perhaps not as we would like to, but we do love you.

Breath of Christ's loving, Holy Spirit, in the depths of our hearts you place the gift of faith – that quite humble trusting in you. So, like the believer in the Gospel, we can say to you "I believe" and at the same time "Come and help my little faith".

Jesus Christ, you came not to judge the world but so that through you, the Risen One, every human creature be saved – reconciled.

And when love that reconciles becomes a fire within us, our hearts, even in the midst of trials, can start to live again.

Jesus Christ, through the Holy Spirit, you are united with every human being without exception.

From each of us you expect a response. If we do not succeed, you know that it is as if there were gaps of unbelief within us. When we welcome you, the Risen One, you open up the way of a communion with you.

Jesus Christ, Love of all loving; you were always within me and I did not realize. You were there and I was not looking for you. Once I had found you, I longed for you to be the whole of my life. A fire was ablaze within me.

But so often, I forgot you again. Yet you kept on loving me.

Living God, we praise you for the multitudes of women, men, young people and children throughout the world who are making their way towards reconciliation.

In the footsteps of all the witnesses of Christ, from Mary and the apostles to the believers of today, enable us to prepare ourselves day after day to place our trust in the Mystery of Faith.

Risen Jesus, from the wellsprings of the Gospel you make goodness of heart and selflessness come surging up inside us, together with that interior harmony which comes from your Spirit within.

And you transfigure our longing, to the point that the simple desire for God is already the beginning of faith.

Jesus Christ, within us there arises a kind of inner voice, and that voice is already prayer.

If our lips remain silent, our hearts listen to you and speak to you.

And you, the Risen One, say to each one of us: surrender yourself quite simply to the life of my Spirit within you; your little faith is enough; I shall never leave you, never.

Jesus Christ, you do not will suffering or distress. And yet we find ourselves in the midst of humanity that is shaken and wounded.

Holy Spirit, Comforter, what we want is not to abandon those who undergo inconceivable trial, and to alleviate the pain of the innocent.

Spirit of the Living God, Holy Spirit, you breathe on what is defenceless and fragile in us. Through you, the valley of tears becomes a place of flowing springs, and your mysterious presence gives the strength to set forth again and again.

Jesus Christ, you were in God from the beginning. From the birth of humanity, you were the Word filled with light. You came among human beings and made the trusting of faith accessible. And the day comes when we can say: I belong to Christ, I am Christ's.

Living God, since your forgiveness is radiant with trust, through you peace of heart is possible and even certain.

The Gospel says: I leave you peace, my peace I give you . . . Through worrying, you cannot add on a single day to your life.

So, for the sake of Christ and the Gospel, you bring us to respond to your call with a yes for the whole of our existence.